Published by **Lion Children's**
www.lionhudson.com
Part of the SPCK Group
SPCK, 36 Causton Street,
London SW1P 4ST

ISBN 978 0 7459 7836 9
e-ISBN 978 0 7459 7989 2

First edition 2022

Acknowledgments
The publisher wishes to thank all the contributors for their involvement in this book, and for their answers.

Getting Started Ch.4; Questions 50, 99, and 101 copyright © 2022 Rosalind Picard
Question 58 copyright © 2022 Matthew Pritchard

The publisher would also like to thank all the children who provided questions.

Scripture quotations taken from the Holy Bible, New International Version Anglicised. Copyright © 1979, 1984, 2011 Biblica, formerly International Bible Society. Used by permission of Hodder & Stoughton Ltd, an Hachette UK company. All rights reserved. "NIV" is a registered trademark of Biblica. UK trademark number 1448790.

This project and publication was made possible through the support of a grant from the John Templeton Foundation. The opinions expressed in this publication are those of the authors and do not necessarily reflect the views of the John Templeton Foundation.

A catalogue record for this book is available from the British Library

Printed and bound in China, November 2021, LH54

101 Great BIG Questions

About God and Science

Brilliant Experts Explore Big Questions from Inquisitive Children

Edited by
Lizzie Henderson and Steph Bryant

LION
CHILDREN'S

BONUS QUESTION:

Why did you write this book?

Have you ever wondered how the universe began, what the point of life might be, or whether God likes science? Every day, we're surrounded by exciting science, lots of ideas about God, and loads of questions about how these things might fit together. We're both Christians who see science as a wonderful gift from God to help us explore some of our big questions about the universe.

All the questions in this book are ones we've been asked by kids just like you. They include some of the biggest, deepest questions that humans have been asking for thousands of years. So we got in touch with some of the very best and brightest people we could think of to help us (and you!) explore them. These experts have spent many years thinking hard about these questions.

Here's a warning: the answers you read are likely to spark even more questions! Our experts would tell you that's a really good thing. Asking questions is one of the things that makes us human. The more we ask, the more we learn. Exploring questions helps us grow in confidence, wonder, and excitement about who we are and our purpose in the universe.

We really hope you enjoy exploring these Great Big Questions. You'll find even more at **www.faradaykids.com** along with activities, videos, and other exciting resources. You can even tell us what you think of this book.

Thanks for reading, keep asking Great Big Questions!

Lizzie Henderson and Steph Bryant (the editors),
Youth and Schools Programme Co-Directors,
The Faraday Institute for Science and Religion, Cambridge, UK

GETTING
PERSONAL:

About the
Editors

Lizzie Henderson
and Steph Bryant,
Youth and Schools
Programme
Co-Directors, The
Faraday Institute for
Science and Religion,
Cambridge, UK

Lizzie and Steph both studied all sorts of interesting science at the University of Cambridge, from rocks, fossils, and evolution (Lizzie's favourites) to wolves and looking after the planet (Steph's favourites). Lizzie and Steph are Christians and love using science to explore the world they believe God made. They also love learning about science, theology, philosophy, and more, especially through exploring Great Big Questions with inquisitive young people. As well as creating resources like this one, they can often be found travelling all around the country to visit young people in schools, churches, and beyond, with a strange assortment of fossils, skulls, chemicals, jelly, pretend wolf poo, funny hats, fairy wings, and all kinds of other exciting things. To learn more about the work Lizzie and Steph do at The Faraday Institute visit **www.faradaykids.com**

Acknowledgments

A huge thank you to all the experts who have contributed their thoughtful and thought-provoking answers to these Great Big Questions. Your encouragement, enthusiasm, grace, humility, and generosity have been invaluable in turning a dream into reality. We also want to say a special thank you to all the young people (and their grown-ups) whom we at Faraday Kids have had the joy of meeting (especially the students at Geddington, Riverview, and Stanion C of E Primary Schools for taking the time to send us some of your very biggest questions while this resource was taking shape), and every young person who has ever been brave enough to voice their big questions. Without your questions, this book would be empty!

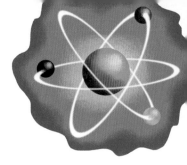

Contents

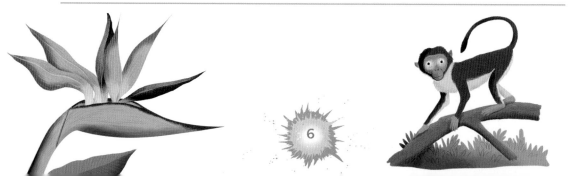

Contents

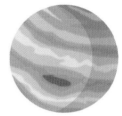

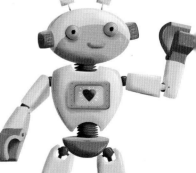

Contents

Chapter 7: Good God? Bad God? 88
Questions About What God is Like

Chapter 8: Friends or Foes? 101
Questions About Science and Religious Faith

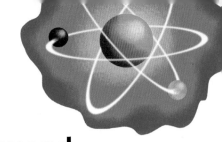

CHAPTER 1

To Infinity and Beyond

Questions About the Beginning, End, and Outside of the Universe

Science works in lots of ways. We talk about using a "method" to do science but it is sometimes hard to say exactly what that method is. Usually it involves noticing something and asking a question, like "How does that happen?"

Sometimes science starts with surprising findings. I once noticed that a liquid made mostly of water unexpectedly turned into stiff jelly overnight. It was a real puzzle, but ideas from other types of science helped us experiment and discover that tiny molecules (groups of atoms) in the liquid had actually joined together into a tangled web.

Sometimes science starts with imagination. At sixteen, Einstein wondered what it would be like to catch a light beam. That curiosity helped him develop an entirely new idea about space and time when he grew up!

Sometimes science starts with maths. Over forty years ago a scientist called Peter Higgs used maths to think about where the mass of stuff comes from. His sums showed that an (undiscovered) particle might be responsible. Forty years later scientists found the "Higgs Particle"!

Sometimes science comes from "playing". Scientists, who knew they could grow crystals in very salty water, wondered what would happen if they added protein molecules. They weren't expecting much but wonderful new crystal shapes appeared! However any particular part of science works, it is always full of exploration, experiments, and wonder.

ETTING
ERSONAL:

/hat inspired
ou to study
pace?

 Jennifer
iseman,
trophysicist

I've been fascinated by space ever since my childhood on a farm. I would wander the country lanes, gazing at the stars filling the night sky wondering what it would be like to visit them! Around then, the first close-up images of our solar system's planets and their moons were being taken by space probes and shown on television. I was amazed by those alien worlds; huge gas planets, and those with rocky rings, icy moons, and possible oceans under the ice. I wanted to be part of the amazing space exploration adventure! I didn't know whether to try to become an engineer, astronomer or even an astronaut! But I did know that I loved nature: forests, lakes, mountains, space, and all animals.

I also learned from my church that nature is God's creation. So studying science seemed a good way to connect with nature and with God. I always felt that scientific study of nature pleases and honours God. I still feel that way. I especially enjoy showing people the amazing things we see and learn about space with our telescopes, and hearing how their lives and faith are enriched by knowing more about our incredible universe.

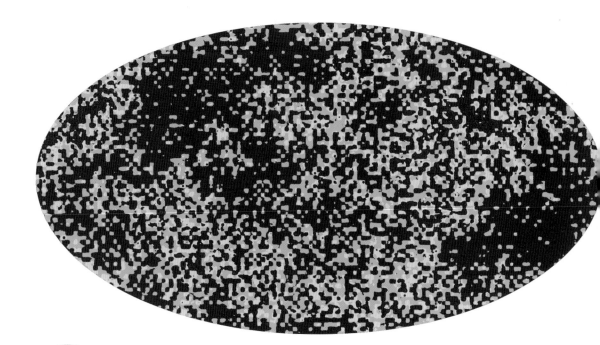

Q1

Where did everything come from? God or the Big Bang?

Hannah Pagel,
Astronomer

When scientists look at the universe, they see that it had a beginning (that we call the "Big Bang"). They see clues that the universe was once infinitely small and they see an afterglow of a beginning, like smoke after a firework show. When Christians look at the universe, they also see a beginning. They share countless stories of the God in which they believe creating everything. Are these different beginnings? Or could they both be true? Couldn't a creator create in any way they choose, even through processes like the Big Bang?

I like to think that scientific studies of the beginning can tell us *how* we're here and religious creation stories can tell us *why* we're here. Science and religion aren't competing to see who has the "right story". I think they're working together, coming at the same story from different angles, helping us to get a more complete picture of the universe.

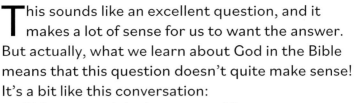

Q2

God made everything, who made God?

The Revd Dr Rodney Holder, cosmologist and theologian

This sounds like an excellent question, and it makes a lot of sense for us to want the answer. But actually, what we learn about God in the Bible means that this question doesn't quite make sense! It's a bit like this conversation:

"Who painted the living room?"

"Mummy painted it."

"Well, who painted Mummy then?"

Just as the painter, Mummy, wasn't painted, so the God who makes everything wasn't made, and anything that was made isn't God.

The Bible tells us that God made absolutely everything, including all of time and space, and that He is different from everything. It tells us that God has always existed, that He existed before there was anything else. So we can think of God as being "outside" time and space, completely different from everything He has created. Just as Mummy with her paintbrush explains why the room is painted, so God explains why the universe exists.

Q3

Is the light mentioned in Genesis the Big Bang?

The Revd Prof. David Wilkinson, astrophysicist and theologian

The first thing God does in Genesis, the first book of the Bible, is say "Let there be light". In the early stages of the Big Bang the universe was filled with electromagnetic radiation (including light). Some have wondered whether the light the Bible is talking about is the light of the Big Bang. But the author of Genesis wouldn't have known about this science. Instead I think they are getting at even bigger ideas than the Big Bang. They talk about light and darkness in a way that feels like a song of worship, exploring and celebrating the idea that God created regular rhythms like day and night, giving sense and stability to our world. Nowadays, we use science to learn more about the rhythms and patterns of the universe, like night and day which come from the earth rotating and orbiting the sun. We call these rhythms the laws of physics and we can thank and praise God for them.

How did everything come from nothing?

Dr Althea Wilkinson,
Astronomer

Science is about searching for answers about bits of our universe that we don't yet understand. People have been exploring parts of this question for a long time, and we think we are beginning to understand some of it. But overall, we still don't know yet!

Science shows that the universe expanded from a tiny point to the size it is today (the Big Bang), so we know that something happened about 13.8 billion years ago bringing time and space into existence. What we haven't worked out yet is quite how it got started. Lots of clever people are using maths, philosophy, physics, and other thinking to develop new theories like "quantum gravity" to try and figure out this exciting mystery.

Perhaps there was never "nothing", or perhaps there was a point when everything came from nothing. We are a long way from finding out, but it's mysteries like this that make science so exciting! And whatever answers we find, I think God loves it when we explore these mysteries of His universe.

Will we ever know exactly how the universe began?

The Revd Prof.
David Wilkinson,
Astrophysicist and
Theologian

There is good evidence that the universe began about 13.8 billion years ago. But we don't yet know what, if anything, started it off (see Q 4). Currently there is a gap in our scientific understanding – a mystery to explore. Some people might think science will never fill this gap and that this is where God comes in, setting off the Big Bang. But this idea could make God very small, just an explanation for things science can't explain yet, and not involved in the rest of time and space. So every new scientific discovery would make God smaller and smaller.

I believe the God of the Bible is the ultimate creator of everything, keeping the whole universe in existence at every moment. I also believe God is involved in all of creation and loves for us to discover more about all He has made. So with every new scientific discovery, I get more and more amazed by God. I can't wait for us to discover more about the universe. If one day we do find out the science behind how the universe began, I will praise God for the wonderful way He creates!

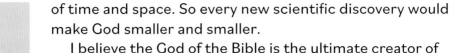

Q6

Why would God make other planets, not just Earth?

Jennifer Wiseman, astrophysicist

We have long known about planets in our solar system. But in recent years, better telescopes have allowed us to detect planets around other stars. We've discovered thousands of these "exoplanets" in our own Milky Way galaxy alone.

Psalm 19 in the Bible says that "the heavens declare the glory of God; the skies proclaim the work of His hands". The writer of this song or poem didn't know all the things we know from science today, but I agree that "glory" – evidence of how awesome God is – can be seen in space, in things like the universe's great size, age, energy, activity, gravity, and beauty.

Space is full of wonderful things – billions of galaxies, each full of countless stars, planets, gassy nebulae, and even new stars forming. Exploring these gives us a sense of God's amazing imagination, generosity, creativity, provision, and power. So God's beautiful and diverse creation – which includes the earth but much, much more, like all the other planets – helps us find out about God who made it.

Q7

Why do theories of creation matter? Surely we should be more concerned about the future?

Dr Deb Haarsma,
Astrophysicist

It's really important to prepare for the future. We should think ahead about all sorts of things, from the changing climate to new medical treatments and how these will affect our world. But it's also important to learn from the past. Do you ever wonder how your parents met? Why they chose the neighbourhood you live in? Maybe you've wondered further back – how did the earth come to be? What were the first people like? In all cultures, people tell stories about the creation of the world and why humans are here. These stories help us think about who we are today, and where we're going.

I think both science and religion help us understand our past and how to move forwards. As a Christian, I believe God created the whole universe, including me and you, and that He loves us as His children. That makes me want to love Him each day and to care for the planet and people He made. I think that the more I learn about where I come from, the better choices I can make about the future.

Q8

hat's
yond the
iverse?

Althea
kinson,
ronomer

Scientists use the word "universe" to mean everything, including all matter, space, and time. So in a way, there is no "beyond", or "outside". That's hard to get your head around because we often imagine the Big Bang like an explosion, but if space and time didn't exist until the Big Bang, then what was it "exploding" out into? Is there anything outside of space and time?

Lots of people believe God created the universe so maybe God is "outside" of time and space. Some people think there are other universes beyond ours. Both these things could be true, but we can't test either with physics. That's because we use science to study things we can observe, and we can only ever see as far as the light from the Big Bang has travelled (the observable universe).

It's very unlikely that we'll ever be able to see "beyond" the edge of our universe, so this question takes us beyond the limits of what science can do. But other types of thinking, like philosophy and religion, can be used to help us explore this extremely big question!

Q9

ould a
ultiverse
ke away the
ed for God?

Andrew B.
rrance,
eologian

The multiverse theory suggests that our universe is one of many within an even larger universe (or multiverse). Some people believe this can explain how our well-ordered universe could have come to exist. So this theory is sometimes said to take away any need to believe in a God who creates and orders our universe.

However, even if we discovered that the multiverse theory is true, it wouldn't mean God would be replaced. We would still need to question where the multiverse (or whatever made the multiverse) came from. Ultimately, if God is creator of everything, the existence of the multiverse would point to God being even more creative than we previously realized. So, for me, the multiverse wouldn't shrink my view of God's creativity; it might even grow it!

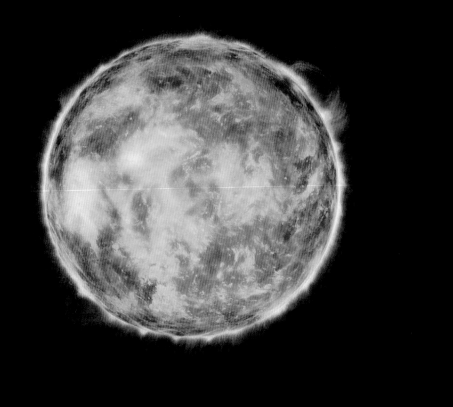

Q10

How and when will the universe end?

Dr Deb Haarsma,
Astrophysicist

We can't know for sure! A wonderful thing about science is that there's always more to learn! Right now, our best science suggests that the universe could expand for ever. If things continue as we see them now, the universe will grow cold, dark, and eventually fade out. But don't worry, that will take trillions and trillions of years. Even our middle-aged sun will keep going for another 5-6 billion years yet!

But there are some other important ideas to think about alongside our science. As a Christian, I believe God started the universe, and that means He's in charge of how and when it ends. I believe the Bible when it says that God will one day make a new heaven and earth. This "new creation" will have no pain or suffering, and people will live in perfect friendship with God. We're not sure what that will look like. But whether it's a whole new universe or a renewal of this one, the Bible tells me it will be wonderful!

Scientists suggest that, in about 5-6 billion years, planet earth will be vaporized as the sun burns out. The end of the universe is even further away and harder to imagine. Scientists have some ideas about how it might happen (see Q 10) but these sound nothing like the apocalypse described in the Bible. That's not surprising: the Bible doesn't give a scientific account of the end of the universe. Instead, it explains what God will do for us and our world when this universe, as we know it, comes to an end.

In biblical terms, "apocalypse" refers to an event in which creation is made new and experiences God's love like never before. We don't know all that this means. But we believe that exploring both scientific and biblical thinking about the universe together helps to paint a bigger picture of what will ultimately happen to creation.

No, the world will carry on. But the way our climate is changing *will* make life very difficult for millions of people, animals, and plants. Recent climate change has mostly been caused by people burning coal, oil, and gas for energy, making the earth hotter than it has been since the Stone Age. As the earth heats up, some places get too hot and dry for plants to grow so people and animals get ill or starve. Thunderstorms become more violent. Ice caps melt. Seas rise. Floods become more common and may wash away homes or drown people and animals.

People living in rich countries often use lots of energy (for cars, houses, aeroplanes etc.) and affect the climate more. But poor people suffer more, especially in poorer countries. Often they can't move away from danger. That's not fair. I believe God loves our world and every plant, animal, and person. We should do all we can to look after our world and help every living thing cope with climate change.

CHAPTER 2

Who Are We and What Are We Doing Here?

Questions About What it Means to be Human

GETTING
STARTED:

**What is
evolution?**

Dr Sarah Bodbyl
Roels,
Evolutionary
Biologist

Evolution happens when the how-to instructions that make living things change over generations. Every cell of each living thing contains a long set of chemical instructions, called DNA.

DNA is copied from biological parents to children. This is why you might look a lot like your parents. Your DNA is a mix of your parents' DNA. But little changes occur in the DNA every time it is copied to a new generation. Over time, generations of little changes may add up to big changes. So groups of living things around today can be quite different from their ancestors of long ago. Just as you are part of a family tree with your parents, grandparents, great-grandparents, and all the generations before them, all living things that have ever existed on Earth are part of one big family tree. Mammoths, mushrooms, hummingbirds, humans, tigers, tyrannosaurs, spiders, and squid are all part of this family. The family of life has become incredibly diverse through lots of little changes over billions of years. Every moment in the history of life has seen a different variety of wonderful living things on our amazing planet.

As a Christian, I love learning about evolution, DNA, and all the processes through which God creates and sustains life. I think the flourishing of life into all kinds of different types, shapes, and colours over billions of years shows God's immense imagination, creativity, patience, and love for His creation.

I care about the environment because I love people, as well as animals and plants, and I want to take good care of them. We all share this planet we call home, so it just makes sense to care about it. Even more than that, I believe God made our world and asked us to look after it. So looking after the environment is an important way of loving God and caring for, protecting, and enjoying what He has given to us.

21

Q13

What is the point of life?

Prof. Cara Wall-Scheffler,
Anthropologist

I think every story I read when I was young was based on this quest – to find the point, or meaning, of life. Books never completely solved it, but the adventures along the way often led the quester to realize something about the importance of love and community.

As anthropologists, we say that our job as a successful species is to continue reproducing. So we could say that the point of life is to get food and water and have healthy children. But doing good, loving others, and making the world a better place are also often seen as important parts of life. Christianity adds to this, teaching that although these are often signs of a life lived with God, they are not the "point" of life. I believe that the true meaning of our lives is to be in full relationship with God.

The Revd Dr Joanna Collicutt,
Neuropsychologist and Theologian

I believe the point of life is to see each moment as a gift, appreciate ourselves for who we are – uniquely created and loved by God – and, from that, realize we can appreciate other people. I believe it means getting involved with the world, playing our part in making it a better place – more like what Jesus called "the kingdom of God".

Dr Jonathan Moo,
ecologist and
theologian

life is all about loving and being loved. I believe Jesus shows us that God made us, knows us, and loves us, and the whole point of our life is to love God back. A big part of that is loving other people, because God loves them too. In fact, God loves the whole universe He made – all of it! We get to spend our life exploring the world God made and learning to love and care for it and for people, just like God does.

Q14

What was God doing before people came along?

Dr Susan D. Benecchi,
planetary Astronomer

I believe that God has always existed and will always exist. I think He created time when He created the universe. So to ask what God was doing "before" that doesn't really make sense, because "before" is a time word and time didn't exist yet! That probably means that God doesn't experience time like we do. Perhaps He can see and experience all of it at once? He's certainly never sitting around waiting for things to happen! But what was God doing between the start of the universe and the first humans? I think He was enjoying creating a universe full of wonderful things!

Prof. Hugh Rollinson,
biochemist

Long before people lived on Earth, I believe God was enjoying making other amazing creatures, and places for them to live. With His amazing creative processes, He shaped and formed the whole universe. On Earth, He used ice to sculpt high mountains, wind to shape the desert dunes, oceans to carve towering cliffs, and rivers to smooth flat plains – all making the beautiful Earth we now get to enjoy exploring.

Q15

Does God like us doing science?

Dr Andrew B. Torrance,
Theologian

The Bible tells us God created humans to rule over the works of His hands (Psalm 8). This is just one of many verses calling us to look after God's creation. To do this, we need to learn all we can about everything God has created. Some of the best ways to do this are with science, so I think God absolutely loves to see us doing science.

Dr Rhoda J. Hawkins,
Biological Physicist

Scientists study nature. Since I believe God made nature, I think God loves us studying it! God gave us brains and wants us to use them well. Science can help us discover new ideas that can be used in medicine or engineering to make life better for others. It can also simply help us to learn more about God's creation and what He's like. So yes, God likes us to do science, learning more about Him, His universe and helping others.

24

Q16

ill God ever
t us discover
erything
out the
iverse?

of. Eric Priest,
thematician

Science is an exciting journey of discovery. I see it as a gift from God. It's amazing to think about the processes in our universe which have led to humans who can spend their lives studying and marvelling at the universe we're a part of. We can learn about our incredible universe every day by reading people's research or through our own experiments, observations, thoughts, and discoveries.

But will we ever discover everything? I don't think so. The universe is vast and the more we discover, the more questions we realize we have still to answer. This process of questioning is central to how science works and it's what makes it so exciting. I think God is thrilled at the discoveries we make with His gifts to us of a wonderful universe and minds to explore it. I'm certain He has plenty more for us to explore!

Q17

an science
er go too far?

Rhoda J. Hawkins,
ological Physicist

We use science to study the natural world. I believe God created everything and finding out more about it is good, so in that sense science cannot go "too far". But sometimes the way we do science or use our scientific knowledge can go "too far", maybe being harmful to people or our world. Special groups called "ethics committees" think carefully about whether to give permission for certain experiments. And it's always important to make sure we use what we learn to help, not harm, God's creation.

of. Paul Fairchild,
em Cell Biologist

From human cloning to artificial intelligence and from nuclear physics to resurrecting ancient dinosaurs, it may seem as if the possibilities of science mean we are bound to stray beyond safe limits. Scientists often have to carefully work out not only what we "could" do, but what we "should" do. "Should" questions don't get answered by science. They are part of something called ethics. I believe we have the power to use science for good or bad and God helps us, but has given us the freedom to make these decisions ourselves. So I think it is important for all of us, whether young or old, to think carefully about ethical questions.

25

Why has God given us the tools to interfere with the universe and "play God"?

Prof. John Bryant,
Geneticist and
Bioethicist

Humans can't change the basic "laws" of the universe. Gravity is still gravity, light is still light, water is still water. But we *can* change other things, especially on Earth.

Why would God let us do that? The Bible tells us that humans are "made in the image of God", which means it is telling us that we are actually God's representatives! I believe God has given us curiosity to discover how the world works, and power and freedom to decide how to use that knowledge. Sometimes we use these tools in ways that hurt others, either deliberately, or because we did something without thinking. I believe it hurts God too when we do that. But I think He loves it when we use these tools to do wonderful things, like using Earth's resources wisely and carefully, caring for living things, and developing cures for diseases. So I believe God lets us "interfere", for good or bad, because He loves us and made us free to make our own choices.

Q19

we evolved
om animals
w can we
responsible
r looking
ter them?

David Lahti,
havioural Biologist

Robert Sluka,
rine Biologist

Q20

o you think
od would
tervene
fore we
stroy the
anet or go
tinct?

Katharine Hayhoe,
mate Scientist

We didn't just evolve from animals, we *are* animals! We're all part of one enormous family! But we're all different. Humans are unique among animals in many ways, including our amazing abilities to make and use complicated tools and advance in technology and new ideas. Our extraordinary intelligence has made us the most powerful animals on Earth, and it allows us to do great good, but also terrible harm. So I think we need to be careful to look after those around us, whether humans or other animals. It's just like the Spiderman movies tell us: with great power comes great responsibility.

I believe the Bible teaches that even now God is actively looking after all He creates, holding everything together so that the universe keeps going. He doesn't need our help. But amazingly, God gives us the gift and responsibility of helping Him. We should always make sure we look after animals and the rest of the world, humbly, responsibly, and wisely, remembering that it's all a gift from God.

Our planet has experienced some very extreme conditions in the past. So we know that, no matter what we do, the planet will survive. But if we don't fix climate change, our civilization might not survive, and that's why scientists like me are so concerned.

God has given us freedom to make choices so I don't think He's going to miraculously reverse what we've done to the planet. But that doesn't mean He can't, won't, or hasn't helped us. He made us creative and imaginative and there are a lot of good choices we can still make to make things better. You could work with your school to cut your carbon footprint, or start talking to your local government about changing things in your town. The most important thing to know is that everyone can make a difference, no matter how young or old!

That depends on what we mean by "powerful". The human brain doesn't take a lot of power to keep going – at full speed, it only needs about 20 watts of power, enough to run a dim light bulb. And it doesn't control all that much muscle power – each brain only has direct control of the body of which it is a part and our bodies are not nearly as powerful as those of lions, gorillas or whales. So by these measures, our brains are certainly not the most powerful things on Earth.

However, a single human brain can make amazing scientific discoveries, create and control powerful technology, tell wonderful, imaginative stories, or explore life-changing ideas of what it means to be human. By this measure, the human brain is indeed one of the most powerful things on Earth! I believe our brains are amazing gifts given to us by God, and we have the responsibility to keep them healthy and use them to further God's purposes in our world. An important question is, how are you going to use yours?

Q22

e my decisions
ntrolled by my
nes, my brain,
something
e?

Francis S. Collins,
neticist

f. Stephanie
rke,
uroscientist

I believe God made us all with free will to make our own decisions. On one level your genes are necessary for this, because they help build the kind of brain that enables you to have free will. But your genes don't directly control your decisions. Your genes and your brain are like an engine for decision-making. But your free will is still needed to "drive the car" and make your decisions.

Our brains are wonderful! My brain makes it possible for me to understand what I see, hear, feel, and smell, and work out what I want. It helps me think about different options, compare ideas, and make choices. So it's an important part of how I make decisions. But it's just one part of me as a whole person. My brain, memories, experiences, beliefs, genes, and much more work together to make the whole "me" which makes my decisions.

Q23

hy didn't God
st make us all
rfect?

e Right Revd Prof.
N. T. Wright,
w Testament
holar

Wouldn't it be simpler if the world were full of perfect people all behaving perfectly towards one another and unable to cause any trouble? The Bible tells us God wanted humans to be His friends. He didn't want to control us like puppets: He wanted us to be able to think for ourselves. Think about it! If someone was *forced* to spend time with you, instead of *choosing* to, would they really count as a friend? So because God loves us so much He even gives us the choice of whether we want to love Him back. But this freedom means we can also choose to do things which aren't loving towards God, others or even ourselves – things which aren't perfect. Christians call this "sin". Amazingly, the Bible tells us that God has made a way to forgive our sin, by becoming human Himself, in Jesus. Jesus chose to love perfectly throughout His human life, death, and resurrection. His choices made it possible for us to be friends with God even though we're not perfect.

Q24

Are religious experiences just in our heads?

Dr Joseph Tennant,
Psychologist

Lots of people would say they have had some kind of religious or mystical experience. Some people have them throughout their entire lives, some have them as part of brain diseases like epilepsy, and some never have anything they would describe that way. These religious experiences are "in our heads". But so are our memories, desires, and feelings.

All human experiences go through our brains, meaning that for all the things we experience and do there is a related electrical signal in our brain. Pain, for example, always comes with an electrical signal in our body. But that doesn't mean it isn't real or doesn't hurt! If we try to limit religion, or anything in human experience, to biology alone, we're missing something.

Any meaning we find in religion comes, not just from the electrical signals in our brains, but from how religion and all our related experiences shape our sense of self, community, and faith. Each person needs to explore that for themselves.

CHAPTER 3

Space Mysteries

Questions About Aliens, Black Holes, Dark Matter, and Time

Stars are like giant factories that make elements – the building blocks of the universe. These factories are weird and wonderful places. They are really, REALLY hot and there is a lot packed into a small space. Inside them, lighter elements like hydrogen and helium can smash together in just the right way to form brand new heavier elements like carbon and oxygen! It'd be like you and your friends throwing golf balls around really fast. When a couple of golf balls collided, you'd suddenly have a tennis ball! Now you start throwing the tennis balls at each other, and you'd get a football! Weird, right?! But that's what stars do!

At the end of their lives, stars send all these new elements shooting out into space. Eventually, these elements can come together with others to form a new star. Sometimes, when a new star forms, the bits left spinning and swirling around it can squish together into planets, like Earth. This means everything on Earth, including the elements that make up our physical bodies, were originally formed within a star! We really are made of star stuff!

I believe God made everything in the universe through these amazing processes. Isn't it incredible to be able to unravel some of these wonderful mysteries behind creation?

GETTING PERSONAL:

What mysteries intrigue you most about life and the universe?

Dr Althea Wilkinson, Astronomer

I am fascinated by beginnings, from the origins of the universe itself to the origins of life. Thanks to science, we now understand lots about the very rapid expansion of space and time at the beginning of the universe. But we really don't understand yet how or why this expansion started (see Q 4 and Q 5). I believe that through science, God lets us learn about how He has made this wonderful place we inhabit, so I'd be excited to discover more about exactly how the Big Bang started! Our scientific developments, like special telescopes, have also allowed us to discover many more planets than those in our solar system. With so many planets orbiting their own stars it seems there are lots of places where life might get going.

I think God loves life – just look at the astonishing amount of life on Earth! So I'd love to know whether there are creatures elsewhere in the universe and whether they also have a relationship with God like we can. Wouldn't it be exciting to make contact with them and see what their big questions are! Maybe in your lifetime we will!

Q25

w much of
e universe
n we visit?

nah Pagel,
onomer

At rocket speed (nearly 25,000 mph), it would take about three months to travel to Mars. To reach Pluto would take over 16 years. And to get to the closest star (apart from the sun) would take about 114,000 years! Light can travel about 27,000 times faster than rockets: it can go around Earth seven times in one second! If we could travel as fast as light (we can't!), it would still take over four years to reach that star. Even at lightspeed, it'd take 2,600 years to reach the farthest star you can see with your eye; 100,000 years to cross our galaxy; and over 13,000,000,000,000 years to reach the farthest objects astronomers have ever seen, which are 76,000,000,000,000,000,000,000 miles away! That's 76 billion trillion miles! Space is absolutely huge! And we might not actually be able to visit much of it, but it is full of exciting mysteries for us to solve!

Q26

How do we know there are things like dark matter in the universe if we can't see them?

Dr Susan D. Benecchi,
Planetary Astronomer

We can't visit much of the universe ourselves (see Q 25). That makes it tricky to explore – a bit like trying to work out what the other end of your street is like without leaving your house. But I believe God has given us science as a gift to explore His wonderful creation. We can make observations on Earth, send spacecrafts to close places, and use telescopes to see faraway things. Sometimes we discover new things by seeing them through telescopes. But sometimes we discover things, not because we see them, but because we see what they do – a bit like the wind which we see only by its effect on things like the leaves of the trees.

Science tells us there are physical laws, like gravity, that seem to always work the same way – on Earth and far out in the universe. But sometimes astronomers make surprising observations that suggest there's something else going on too – things we can't see but that affect our measurements and observations, like invisible puzzle pieces. Dark matter is the name scientists use for a possible type of invisible matter that could explain some of the strange things affecting what we see. Some scientists suggest that as much as 95 per cent of the universe might be invisible puzzle pieces! Science has helped us solve lots of mysteries in the past and the more we learn, the closer we get to figuring out these puzzles.

34

Q27

hy do people
ink Earth is
special?

Sarah Bodbyl
els,
lutionary
logist

ah Walker,
ironmental
mmunicator

. Stephen
land,
obiologist

Earth is just the right distance from the sun to have liquid water. Scientists think that is part of what allowed life to develop here – and not just a few tiny living things, but a teeming bounty of life! Life in all different types, colours, and shapes, found everywhere on the planet and continually changing throughout history through incredible evolutionary processes. That's pretty special!

Our world is an amazing place filled with wonderful things! Just last year, in Ghana, we discovered a White-naped Mangabey – an endangered monkey no one knew existed there! I believe that all creatures are precious and deeply loved by God. I am honoured to play my small part in caring for them, so that they can thrive and have their own special relationships with Him.

One way to think about Earth being special is that it seems different from anywhere else. With better and better telescopes, we have found more and more planets, many of which are "Earth like", but there's lots to do to work out just how similar they might be. So far, Earth is the only planet known to have life, and many of the things that seem to make Earth special are to do with that life. We used to think that life got started here because Earth was different. But now it seems that life has actually produced lots of those differences! It may well be that we find life on other planets in the next few years and if we do, it's unlikely to be quite the same as us. So there are still lots of reasons to think that Earth is special, but other places might be just as special in their own way!

Q28

Are there any other planets like Earth? Could we live on another planet?

Dr Hannah Earnshaw,
Astronomer

In our solar system, there are rocky planets close to the sun and huge gas giants further away. No others are quite like Earth. Astronomers have now discovered thousands of planets around other stars, including types we don't have, like "super-Earths" ten times the size of Earth! But to see if one could support life, we need to look for signs of things that make life on Earth possible, like a rocky surface, oxygen to breathe, and liquid water. Living on another planet without these conditions would be very challenging, but scientists are already exploring how humans could live on nearby Mars. We'd need to produce our own air, water, food, and building materials from what is available on the planet's surface. It's important to remember that, wherever we live, we must take care of the environment. I think humans could live on Mars one day. But I also believe God has called us to look after Earth – after all, as far as we know, there is only one planet quite like it!

Q29

Should we really be exploring space when there are still problems on Earth?

Jennifer Wiseman, Astrophysicist

Every person and every country has to make big choices about how they want to use their time, money, and effort. We can put it into solving problems like disease, poverty, and war, and also into developing "good" things, like music, art, and expanding knowledge. Both areas are important things to focus on and I think we need a mix of both because focusing on the good things helps us to have hope, energy, enthusiasm, and creativity to solve the problems. Exploring space helps us develop science and technology that can help other good human activities and needs. It also helps us pause in wonder by giving us a sense of how we fit into an amazing universe. I believe this is part of God's gift to help us look after His creation.

Q30

What are black holes? What's inside them?

George Hawker, Astrophysicist

Jump. What happens? On Earth, you'll come right back down. That's because both you and Earth have mass (you're made of matter). Mass is attracted to other mass by a force called gravity. The more mass packed into an object, the stronger its pull of gravity. If you could jump fast enough (like a rocket) you could overcome Earth's gravity, and you wouldn't come down! Rockets go about 11,000 metres a second but there is something much faster! Light travels at 299,792,458 metres a second! The famous scientist Albert Einstein worked out that nothing can travel faster than light.

But what's this got to do with black holes? A black hole is an object where a *huge* amount of mass is packed into a tiny bit of space! That means the pull of gravity is so strong, not even light is fast enough to get out of it. So from outside, black holes look completely dark and there's no way of knowing exactly what's inside them. All we know is there must be so much mass packed in there that its matter has collapsed in on itself! Sound weird? It is! What an exciting mystery to explore!

Could a black hole crush Jesus?

The Revd Prof. David Wilkinson, Astrophysicist and Theologian

Black holes are exciting, but not a good place to visit! As you approach a black hole, the gravitational forces are so strong that any human being would be stretched out like spaghetti and ripped apart! Not much fun!

Christians believe that Jesus came into the world as both God and a human being. I think part of that meant that He experienced life just like any other human – tiredness, hunger, pain, and the force of gravity. So, just like any other human, He would be pulled apart if He went too near a black hole.

Now there were some occasions in Jesus' life when He resisted gravity, like when He walked on the Sea of Galilee. But these were rare and deliberate events – to teach us that God was at work in the world. So He probably could resist the gravity of a black hole if He wanted to, but we don't have any evidence to tell us that He ever went near enough to do so!

Q32

we stood at
e edge of a
ack hole and
oked back at
rth would
e see back
time?

dy Fletcher,
ence
mmunicator

To understand black holes, we have to think about gravity (see Q 30), and this is where gravity gets weird! Scientists and mathematicians think of space and time together as "space-time". We can think of space-time a bit like the surface of a trampoline. Objects made of matter bend space-time, just like you would bend a trampoline if you stood on it. This bending of space-time is what gravity is. The greater an object's mass the more it bends space-time and so the greater its gravity. Think about how much more the trampoline would be bent by a bowling ball than by a tennis ball! Because time is bent as well as space, the closer you are to the centre of a massive object, the slower time passes. It's weird to think about, but that means that time passes a tiny bit more slowly at the centre of the earth than at the top of Everest.

Black holes are very dense and heavy, so bend space-time a lot and have enormous gravity. So as you get closer to a black hole, time moves very, very slowly. That means that as you looked back at the earth, you would actually see time moving much more quickly than it seemed to for you. You could even think of it as a bit like looking *forward* in time!

Of course, we couldn't actually get near a black hole without becoming shredded spaghetti, but isn't it amazingly interesting and weird to think about the puzzles of our amazing universe that science helps us to uncover!

**Do aliens
exist? If so,
what are
they like?**

Prof. Stephen
Freeland,
Astrobiologist

Scientists haven't discovered any aliens yet, but neither do we know that they don't exist! Scientific findings suggest our universe is far more "life-friendly" than we once thought. We have learned that there are loads of planets; that life on Earth got started quickly, using the most common types of atoms in the universe – carbon, hydrogen, oxygen, and nitrogen; and that life thrives in many Earth environments where we thought life would be impossible. So I wouldn't be surprised if we do find alien life in the universe.

But what might aliens look like? Since Earth life is made from the most common types of atoms, the chances are that any other life in the universe would be too. So if they do exist, aliens might be weirdly similar to life on Earth. Of course, most life on Earth is (and has been) tiny, single-celled squishy things like bacteria. So the chances are, any life we find elsewhere would be too. But it's certainly not impossible that somewhere out there are aliens a bit like you and me!

**Does God
know or
care about
aliens? Why
doesn't the
Bible mention
them?**

The Revd Dr
Andrew Davison,
Theologian and
Scientist

I believe God made everything, and He knows and loves all of it. So, if there are aliens (and it now seems more likely than it used to – see Q 33), that includes them too. I think aliens aren't mentioned in the Bible simply because that isn't what the Bible is trying to tell us about. I believe God revealed some things to the people who wrote the Bible, but He didn't download a whole scientific history of the universe to them. There are lots of things the Bible doesn't tell us about - penguins, pterodactyls, planets, plankton, and plenty more! God's given us science to explore these exciting parts of our world.

I think God shared even more important things with the Bible writers. He taught them about Himself, us, what He's done, and how much we need Him. So, although the Bible doesn't mention aliens, that doesn't mean they're not there, or not important. The Bible is just focused on other things. But I think the Bible does show us that God's love and knowledge reach everywhere, including to any aliens!

Q35

ould scovering ens stop u believing God?

Hannah Earnshaw, ronomer

The millions of strange and wonderful species on Earth, alive today or in prehistoric times, show me that God is an incredibly inventive creator. We don't yet know if life exists on other planets, but we do know that there's space for it! There are probably billions of planets around other stars in our galaxy (see Q 28) and God is definitely creative enough.

The Bible suggests that God understands and relates to creatures in a special way that humans can't - even using examples of some strange creatures like leviathan and behemoth, which we're not sure were real or legendary. This reminds me that even things that are outside our understanding are not outside God's. So, I think it is perfectly possible that there might be creatures, and maybe even people, on other planets, that are made, loved, and understood by God. And if they do exist, discovering aliens wouldn't stop me believing in God; they'd just be one more thing that points to God's unlimited creativity.

Could Jesus time travel?

Andy Fletcher,
Science Communicator

I believe Jesus came to Earth as a human and is also God. That gives us some interesting questions about what He could do (see Q 31). We may never be able to "time travel" like we see in the movies. But technically, we are all constantly moving forwards in time, which is pretty cool when you think about it!

Einstein's Special Theory of Relativity describes something amazing: the faster you go, the slower time passes. So if you travelled really fast in a spaceship, you'd age more slowly than your friends on Earth. When you came back, your friends (who were your age when you left) would be older than you! It would be as if you'd time travelled into the future.

As far as the Bible tells us about His time on Earth, Jesus never went on a rocket. But I believe that Jesus, as God, is creator of the universe and inventor of time, space, and even the speed of light. So I think He can be everywhere and everywhen with everyone, all at the same time. That's not just time travel. It's time and space travel in all directions for all of space and all of time. Pretty awesome!

CHAPTER 4

Where Did We Come From and Where Are We Going?

Questions About the Origins and Future of Humanity

GETTING
STARTED:

Digital brains
What is
artificial
intelligence?

Prof. Rosalind
Picard,
Computer Scientist
and Inventor

It might sound strange but this is something about which even artificial intelligence researchers don't all agree! We're mostly trying to create something in machines that seems to be similar to, or as good as, *human* intelligence. Humans generally rely on information we gather through our senses, especially our eyes and ears. Some researchers focus on developing machines that use cameras and process visual data a bit like we do, while some work on programming computers to recognize and respond to speech. These computers might be able to process data to "recognize" a face, words or sentences, or display "emotions". But they're not really "intelligent" like we are. They don't understand what a face is or have feelings, emotions or experiences. Underneath, it's just software and hardware designed by humans.

All this development is exciting. It could help us communicate better or look after each other well. But it could also be used to hurt or control people. Humans are in control of the technology, so I think we need to make sure that we focus on loving each other and the world well, and be careful about building technology that makes people's lives better.

My science constantly adds to how amazed I am by humanity. I got a real sense of awe when leading the Human Genome project, which uncovered the three billion letter genetic code in the DNA of each of our cells. We continue to learn more about the ways in which that DNA code builds wonderful human beings who live, breathe, and interact with the world around them. I find that breathtaking.

I also find it amazing how, through the processes of evolution gradually adapting and changing this DNA code, humans have developed minds that can now question, explore, and understand so much about the world and the God who I believe made it all. Scientific research and exploration provide a chance for me, as both a scientist and a believer, to wonder at and worship God and celebrate the humans He loves so much.

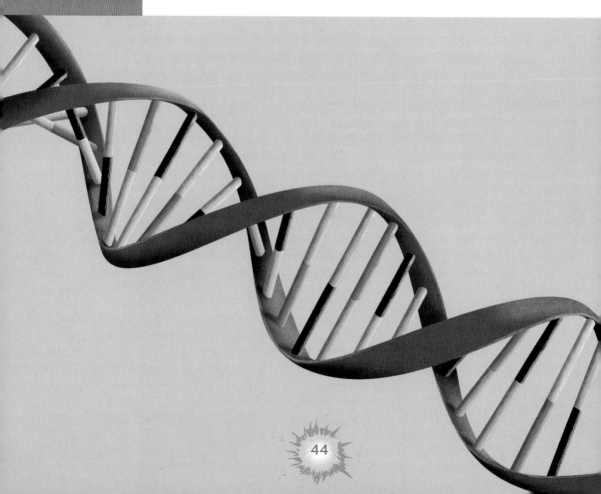

Q37

hat makes
e me?

Francis S.
lins,
neticist

Revd Dr Joanna
licutt,
ropsychologist
Theologian

f. Tom
kespeare FBA,
iologist,
adcaster, Social
uencer

Lots of things contribute to who you are. The DNA you inherit from your biological parents, the environment you grow up in, your experiences and opportunities all help to shape you in certain ways. But what really makes you you is the combination of all those things, plus your life choices. You become the unique person you are through the choices you make every day.

No two people are exactly the same – not even identical twins! Some important differences include our names, the things we like (food, music etc.), what we think is important, how we look, how we move, our funny little habits, where we call home, and the story of our lives. Above all I think what makes us who we are is who we love, and who loves us. For many of us, including me, God is a big part of that.

My genes, my upbringing, my education, my social background, gender, ethnicity, disability, and sexuality, the thousands of people I have met, the mistakes I have made, the chances I have taken and the experiences I have had, all combine to make me the unique and unrepeatable person I am. I believe we are made by God, wonderfully complex, and made up of so many different things.

Modern Gorilla · Modern Human · Homo Erectus · Australopithecus Africanus · Modern Chimpanzee · Modern Bonobo

Gorilla Ancestry · Human Ancestry · Chimpanzee Ancestry · Bonobo Ancestry

8-19 million years ago · 6-7 million years ago · 2 million years ago

Q38

Where did the first humans come from?

Dr Dennis Venema,
Geneticist

Science tells us humans evolved slowly, through lots of little changes (see Chapter 2 "Getting Started"), so it is difficult to say who the "first" humans were. But we can think about where they came from.

If you went back in time about 6 or 7 million years to meet your long-ago ancestors, they wouldn't look much like you. But the descendants of this ancient species divided into groups that gradually became quite different. One group eventually became chimpanzees, and another became humans. Fossils help us see how, over many generations, our ancestors began walking upright, making stone tools, creating art, and their average brain sizes became larger. Eventually they became so much like us that we call them "human"!

We can explore when some of these important changes happened. The oldest fossil people found (so far) with skeletons like ours lived in Africa about 350,000 years ago. But they didn't do all the things modern humans do: they didn't grow crops, farm animals, or make art like we do. By about 50,000 years ago, when humans left Africa and spread into the rest of the world, people were doing all those "human" activities. Exploring fossils from between these dates helps us learn about the fascinating development of our species.

Q39

ve evolved,
w can we be
de by God?

Denis Alexander,
chemist

The Bible says God created, and is still creating, everything. And I believe science is a gift to help us study the processes He uses. So I think evolution is the wonderful process God uses to make us and all other living things! I think of God creating things like an author creates a novel. The whole book is written by the author, gradually, over time, from beginning to end. Nothing happens in the novel without the author being involved. I think of God as the author of everything that exists – the whole story of creation – from the beginning to the end of time… even beyond!

Science is wonderful because it helps us explore God's exciting novel of creation. It helps us see that evolution is a really important theme running through the whole story. I believe it is the part of the story that tells us how God makes all living things. God's novel is the story of one huge family, all related to each other, throughout history. Each of God's creatures has a long family history, connecting it to everything that has ever lived on Earth! Humans are part of that creation – related to all God's other amazing living things through our evolutionary history. And we have our own very special part to play – we are the only creatures who can learn to read God's novel of life. What a great privilege!

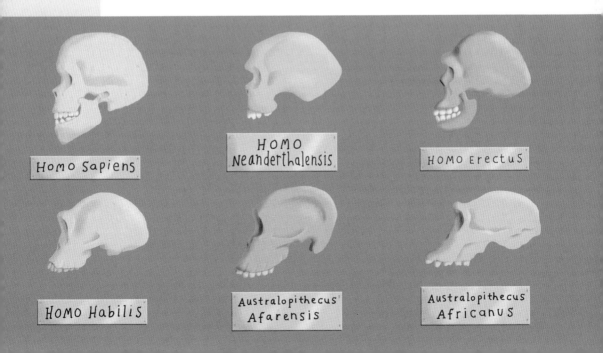

Homo Sapiens

HOMO
Neanderthalensis

HOMO Erectus

HOMO Habilis

Australopithecus
Afarensis

Australopithecus
Africanus

Spoiler! We did not evolve from chimpanzees, as people sometimes think. Science actually shows that we evolved from a type of ape that probably looked a bit like a cross between a chimpanzee and a gorilla. When and where? About 6 or 7 million years ago in Africa (see Q 38). At that point in our history the ancestors of chimpanzees began to develop in a particular way and have lived in the African jungle ever since. Human ancestors developed in a different way. Soon they walked on two legs, became skilled toolmakers, and importantly developed large brains.

Human history shows the same pattern we see through the rest of evolutionary history. Through tiny changes in each generation adding up to big differences over thousands and millions of years (see "What is evolution?" p. 20), wonderful new species arise all the time. Sooner or later nearly all species go extinct and are replaced by amazing new species. Many human-like species have existed, most famously the Neanderthals, but apart from ourselves all have now vanished – mostly by extinction, but also because sometimes one species of human evolved into another. Now our closest living cousins are chimpanzees, who have their own history since they branched off from us all those millions of years ago, but curiously, they seem to have changed less than we humans.

Q41

...ho were
...am and
...e? Were
...ey real?

Elspeth Darley,
...chologist and
...ologian

The Bible begins with some stories about where everything came from, including humans. One story talks about man being made from the ground and called "Adam", which is Hebrew for "ground" and "man" – original hey? The story then says God made woman, called "Eve", meaning "living", and the two got together and populated the planet. Right? These stories can raise some important questions for us, especially as science suggests that humans evolved slowly over time (see Q 38, Q 39, and Q 43). Some Christians think Adam and Eve were real people; others think they might just represent people in general.

But I don't actually think that whether or not they were real is the most important question. I believe that sometimes, things can tell us true things without being real. If I said, "It's raining cats and dogs" you would understand the truth that it is raining a lot, but you wouldn't think it was really raining animals. So just because Adam and Eve might not have been real doesn't mean the story about them can't be true. I believe that the story tells us lots of true things including: God created humans, humans were made to be friends with God, and humans broke that friendship but God still loved them. So I think the point of the story was really to communicate that God made you at your best and loves you at your worst.

think it is helpful to think of the stories at the start of Genesis as a bit like the stories Jesus told – written to teach us spiritual and moral truths about God and our relationship with Him, rather than necessarily to talk about historical events (see Chapter 5 "Getting Started"). I think the story of God giving Adam and Eve clothes tells us lots about our relationship with God. It says that when Adam and Eve did what God said was good for them, they lived in a comfortable place and were naked with no shame. But when they chose to do their own thing instead, they felt uncomfortable about being naked. I think this might represent their shame at having disobeyed God, just as we feel exposed and vulnerable when we realize we've behaved badly or let someone down.

The story says God was sad they had disobeyed Him, because their relationship couldn't be the same any more, but He gave them clothes. This shows that God cares for our physical needs. In the story, because of Adam and Eve's disobedience they had to leave a comfortable place and go where they would need protection from things like thorns and thistles. God also gave them clothes so they wouldn't have to feel ashamed of their nakedness. This shows God cares for our emotional and spiritual needs even after we disobey Him.

The story doesn't say what would have happened if Adam and Eve hadn't disobeyed God. It is certainly hard to imagine living in many places without clothes to keep us warm, dry, and protected! But I think the clothes in the story are actually a picture of God's care for us.

Q43

...ve evolved
...e all other
...imals, why do
...ople think we
...e so special?
...hat makes us
...fferent from
...her animals?

...Steve Roels,
...ironmental
...ogist

...f. Cara
...ll-Scheffler,
...hropologist

Humans evolved like other animals, but we seem different somehow, don't we? No other species builds hospitals, goes to space, or communicates in writing like I am doing with you. Animals show different kinds of intelligence, but human intelligence allows us to do things other animals cannot. Christians believe God gave humans this intelligence so we can have a special relationship with God, different to God's relationship with other animals. We can know God personally and have moral responsibilities that other animals do not have.

Humans can seem special or different for lots of reasons: we can know right from wrong, have long-term friendships, and make complex art that we think of as "beautiful". We need to be careful that we don't ignore the wonderful and clever things that other animals can do, but I think we do see some differences in the way humans behave. One special thing is our ability to make something like a sculpture or a story about something we've never seen before – that is, to have imagination. Imagination has been an important part of human development and we only see evidence of imaginative art among *Homo sapiens* so I think it sets us apart.

What does the Bible mean when it says we are "made in the image of God"?

Dr J. Richard Middleton,
Theologian

The Bible says God made humans "in His image". But that doesn't mean we physically look like God. I think it describes the mission God has given us: to get to know Him in a special way and represent Him in the world. What does that look like? Well, although we can't literally see God, the Bible says He created the entire universe and loves everything He made – people, animals, plants, ecosystems, even stars and galaxies. So I think that when we love each other and look after this beautiful universe and the creatures that live here, we show God's love to the world. I believe we represent God by acting as He does.

It is also interesting that when the first part of the Bible was written, the phrase "image of god" was used to describe statues of gods and also powerful kings – not ordinary people. It meant that the statue or king was very special because they had the authority and responsibilities of a god. When the Bible says ALL people are made in God's image, I think it is saying how special God thinks all people are, and how much responsibility He gives us, to live and love like He does.

Q45

d souls
olve?

f. Malcolm Jeeves,
chologist

This is a huge, mysterious question which has long captivated people trying to work out what makes each person feel like "me". And there have been many different ideas! For thousands of years, people thought of the soul as some mysterious non-physical part hidden somewhere within each of us. One idea, called the "Hebrew view", suggested that our minds, bodies, and souls are closely tied together into a whole being. Another, called the "Greek view", claimed that the soul was separate and "lived in" the body.

Today, most leading biblical scholars agree that when we talk about the "soul" we are actually talking about our mind and body combined into a whole person. For example, you might have heard people talk about a "village of two hundred souls", simply meaning two hundred people. Interestingly, scientists have found that the mind and brain are very closely linked together, and our understanding of evolutionary biology and psychology also suggests that our bodies and minds are closely linked. So to find out how everything that makes you "you" has evolved, we can keep exploring how evolutionary processes have shaped the way our brains and bodies work. But there is a lot we don't yet know, and there are always more questions to explore. So watch this space!

Is it human nature to believe in God?

Prof. Justin L. Barrett,
Developmental Psychologist

Yes, studies show belief in God is *almost* entirely natural. It is natural to look around at plants, animals, mountains, and rivers, wonder what they are for and whether someone made them that way. It seems easy for kids to think about God's special powers, like being able to see, hear, and know things that people can't. In fact, studies show four-year-olds may find it easier to naturally understand some ideas about God than those about humans – children in the UK, the Dominican Republic, Kenya, and Mexico got more answers right about what God's abilities would allow Him to know than about what their human friend could know.

So, it seems humans naturally think about God and His "superpowers". Things we learn from parents and religious leaders build on this. But what different people learn as they grow up might mean they end up believing different things about God, even whether He is real. The Bible says God is real and wants to be friends with us, so I think it makes sense that He would make it natural to believe in Him.

Q47

ve humans opped olving?

Francis S. Collins,
neticist

April Maskiewicz
rdero,
logist

We are still evolving. We see that in things like the way changes in DNA have made some people in certain parts of the world more resistant to particular illnesses, or able to tolerate certain diets or climates. But it is harder to spot changes happening now because they happen really slowly, and we travel more. Groups of people don't tend to live in one place and adapt to it over time like we used to. We also have wonderful things like medicine and social care, which mean that illnesses and disabilities have less impact than they used to. So we can't see human evolution happening in our own experience, but we are definitely still evolving.

All species are constantly evolving. When DNA gets copied and passed down to the next generation, little copying mistakes always happen, making changes to the DNA code. Some of these changes are helpful and continue getting passed down from generation to generation. Others that are unhelpful can mean that the animal or plant with that DNA won't survive as long or pass on these changes. Some people think that improvements in medicine might have stopped human evolution, but the human population is always evolving. Scientists have discovered many little changes to human DNA over time that have helped us in lots of different ways. For example, a long time ago, a little change in the DNA copying of one of our ancestors allowed them to digest lactose, the stuff found in milk products. This got passed on, so if you enjoy milk and ice cream, then you have evolution to thank!

Q48

How will we change in the future?

Dr Beth Singler,
Anthropologist

Dr Michael S. Burdett,
Theologian and
Philosopher

Science fiction shows us some interesting ideas people have had about how we might change in the future, and real technologies such as artificial intelligence (AI) can also inspire predictions. We often think mechanical minds might help us to do things faster and better. Studying AI might even help us understand more about how our bodies and minds work. Whatever happens, I think humans are likely to keep being tool-users: shaping technology, and also being shaped by it.

Do you like using smart phones or tablets? What do you use them for? Playing games, calling your friends? Some people think these exciting technologies could be built into our bodies in the future and make our wildest dreams possible – we might live longer, be smarter or more friendly. However we change in the future, I don't think technology can do everything. I believe humans will still need Jesus Christ in order to live the best lives God has for us.

Q49

**uld humans
r become
ermaids?**

Steve Roels,
ironmental
ogist

In theory, yes! Humans could evolve into mermaids, assuming "mermaid" means a semi- or fully-aquatic life form and doesn't require underwater kingdoms or singing crab friends! The evolutionary change from living on land to living partly or entirely in water has happened several times. Seals, whales, penguins, turtles, and even extinct mosasaurs all came from ancestors that lived on land! However, past evolutionary shifts from land to water took millions of years and happened under certain environmental conditions that humans might never experience.

Predicting the direction of evolution is always tricky because of the interaction of little genetic changes with the environment and animal behaviour. But with humans it is even more complicated because our culture and technology come into play. This makes it seem less likely we will evolve into mermaids. For example, native people in Alaska have hunted seals and whales for thousands of years but they didn't evolve flippers – they invented kayaks. That might sound less exciting, but our clever ways of thinking have allowed us to do amazing things, including taking different routes to life on, or in, the water, asking Big Questions and even telling imaginative stories about things like mermaids.

Q50

Will robots get cleverer than people and take over?

Prof. Rosalind Picard,
Computer Scientist and Inventor

No! Film makers love to paint a picture of robots dramatically taking control and outsmarting humans. But robots are built by and for people, so people are ultimately in control of what robots do, and what they're able to do, whether good or bad. Robots are programmed to be better at some tasks than people. Some can store much more information than humans can remember, or do more complicated or speedier calculations, but that doesn't mean they're cleverer than us or will ever be able to take over. As we get better at programming robots so that we can interact with them more naturally, they may seem more like us, or even cleverer in some tasks. But human "cleverness" is much more than information storage or doing something that we were taught to do. No matter how well we might program them to seem as if they do, robots don't "know", "feel", "experience" or "decide" anything unless it is programmed into them, so it's very unlikely they could "take over" from humans.

Q51

**...uld a robot
...er fall in love
...e people
...or have
...ligious faith?**

...f. John Wyatt,
...dical Doctor
... Ethicist

Artificial intelligence (AI) is very different from how humans think and feel. Deep emotions like love and worship seem closely related to what it means to be human, including how our bodies function. So I find it hard to imagine technology that would let a robot have similar experiences. Robots we currently have or can imagine cannot experience pain, joy, love or fear like humans can. Advanced technology may allow robots to simulate human emotions – a robot could be programmed to say "I love you" in such a caring way that you might believe it. But there's a big difference between a robot programmed to say "I love you" and a human who *chooses* to say it.

Christianity and other religions teach that humans are special because we can relate to God in a special way. I don't think machines can experience that. It is, of course, possible that in the future a super-advanced AI might be capable of feeling emotions or having some awareness of God's existence. We don't know what the future might hold!

Will science one day help people live forever?

Dr Michael S. Burdett,
Theologian and Philosopher

One amazing thing science can do is help us explore how our bodies change as we get older. The older we get, the more easily we get sick, break bones, and get tired. Often these things happen because the tiny building blocks of our bodies, called cells, stop working as well or even shut down completely when they get too old.

Scientists are trying to work out how to keep cells working well and stop them shutting down. If they can, it might mean we could live longer and healthier lives in the future. That's exciting! But even if we could keep our bodies going, we still wouldn't actually be able to live forever because the lifetime of our sun and even the universe itself is limited (see Q 10 and Q 11).

As a Christian, I think it's great to use science to help us stay healthy for longer, but I think there's something better than keeping our bodies going forever. Death is sad, but I believe God has promised we can live with Him forever in a new way after we die (see Q 90). I think that's even more exciting than what His wonderful gift of science can offer!

CHAPTER 5

A Day in the Life of God

Questions About God, People, and Religion

ETTING
ARTED:

ho wrote
e Bible?
n we
ally believe
erything
says?

e Revd Dr
est Lucas,
lical Scholar

The Bible was written by lots of different people over more than a thousand years. It is made up of 66 different books and we don't know who wrote them all! Lots of books were written by early followers of Jesus like James, John, Luke, Paul, and Peter, and we know quite a lot about these writers. The books of prophets like Isaiah and Ezekiel record their messages from God to groups of people, but they were sometimes written by someone collecting what the prophet said and adding details about the prophet's life. And some books are named after major characters in the story like Joshua, Ruth, or Samuel but we don't know who wrote them.

Christians believe God inspired and guided the writers of the Bible so that it contains reliable spiritual and moral truth. But one of the exciting things about the Bible is that it contains many different kinds of writing, including historical accounts, stories and parables, poetry, songs, wise sayings, prophecies, letters, logical arguments, and visions. Each kind of writing expresses truth in different ways. For example, the Gospel books (Matthew, Mark, Luke, and John) are eyewitness accounts of Jesus' life, death, and resurrection, and we can trust that these events actually happened. But when the psalmist (songwriter) says that God rescued him from a muddy pit and put his feet on a rock he's not necessarily saying that's exactly what God did, but explaining that God delivered him from a difficult situation. So working out the kind of writing and the way it communicates truth is really helpful and sensible for understanding and trusting what each part of the Bible says.

GETTING PERSONAL:

Why are science and faith both important to you?

Dr Tom Ingleby,
Geophysicist

I've always loved building stuff – with Lego as a child, and now with wood. I get to be creative, learn how things work, and maybe even build something helpful for people. Science is a great way of doing those things too: I get to explore and think of new ways to explain how the world works and help improve people's lives. When I was a teenager, I thought of God in a similar way: He was a good explanation for why we were here and some of the things He said seemed to improve people's lives.

University was a really important time in my life. I met the woman I married! I discovered that I loved geology – the study of Earth and its history – science was more exciting than ever! And I also met Jesus – not in person, but as I read about Him in the Bible, God was no longer just an explanation, but an exciting, powerful, and loving person I could get to know!

As I learned more about Jesus, I had loads of questions about how science and Christianity fit together. The great thing was that I knew thoughtful people who had good answers to those questions. They helped me see that science and Christianity fit together wonderfully. I learned to see science as an amazing gift from God that allows us to learn more about His remarkable universe, helping us take good care of it and everyone who lives in it. Science and faith are both so exciting. I love helping others explore how they fit together!

n science
ove God's
istence?

Revd Dr
ian Straine,
sicist and
ologian

The short answer is "No!". That might seem disappointing, but it actually shows us something pretty amazing about God. Science is the study of the physical world. Scientists explore nature, do experiments, use maths, and do other things to learn about our amazing universe, down to the tiniest particle (see Chapter 1 "Getting Started").

While the Christian faith is clear that God is creator of the whole universe, I think God is outside of this physical universe so He cannot be "measured" scientifically. Instead, people usually look at other important kinds of evidence to explore God's existence, like their experiences of prayer, how worship makes them feel, how Christianity makes sense of difficult questions, the trustworthy nature of the Bible's accounts of Jesus – even the idea that only God could create such a beautiful universe with patterns and "laws" we can explore with science!

How can God exist outside of space and time?

The Revd Dr
Rodney Holder,
Cosmologist and
Theologian

We have only ever existed within space and time so it is hard for us to understand anything existing outside of them. But the Bible tells us God can do this because He is different from everything He has created, including all of space and time!

One way to think about it is to imagine a creature called a splatbody that is totally flat. It has no height at all, only length and width. It moves about on a flat surface bumping into other splatbodies. It can't really understand or describe a bird soaring around in the sky above it because it doesn't understand "up and down", only forwards, backwards, and sideways! We can think of ourselves as a bit like the splatbody, and God as (a bit) like the bird, existing outside of what we can really understand. But the bird could fly down and touch the splatbody. Christians think God can touch us too, living inside each of us, as the Holy Spirit, if we let Him. The Bible also says God loves us so much that He came down to Earth as Jesus so that we could understand Him better. A bit like the bird becoming a splatbody!

Q55

s God left
is He still
olved in
eation?

onathan Moo,
ogist and
ologian

Sometimes people wonder whether God "kick-started" creation and then left us to get on with it. But I don't think that's true at all! I do believe God has given us lots of responsibility – asking us to show love and kindness to others and care for creation. We have the power to do lots of good, but also lots of damage. But the Bible says God is still here, holding everything together, giving life to everything, and helping us. I think even the good work we do, like using ecology to work out the best way to restore damaged parts of creation, is only possible because God gives us the ability to do it. In fact, I believe God's love means He not only holds the world together but promises to one day make it new and fix the mistakes we have made. The Bible says we see this promise in Jesus who, as God, became part of creation by becoming human, defeating the evil in the world, and giving us new life. I think Jesus shows us for sure that God didn't just make everything and then leave.

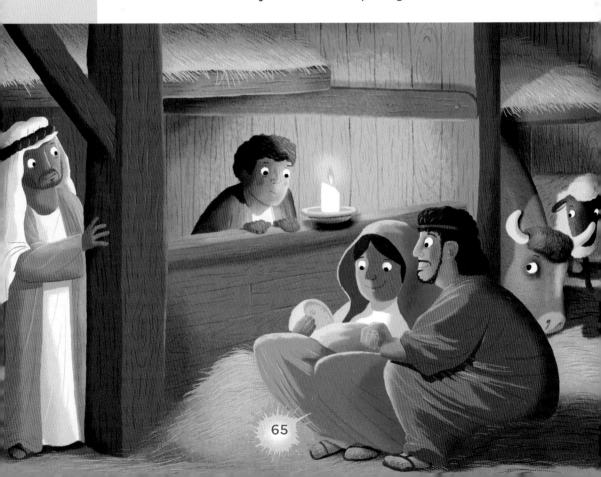

Q56

Is the human brain capable of understanding God?

Prof. Stephanie Clarke,
Neuroscientist

I believe God made everything, including us, and wants us to know Him. But what does it mean to "understand God"? It could mean knowing about who God is, what He has done, and how great He is. It could also mean knowing Him personally – trusting, loving, and worshiping Him.

The human brain is well equipped for learning. We can explore what the Bible teaches and do things like science to learn about God and the universe I believe He has created. We can also use our brains to store personal memories, make decisions, reason, love, trust, and appreciate family and friends. So I think humans are certainly capable of knowing lots of things *about* God, and also knowing Him personally. But some things we learn about God are very hard for us to fully "understand" because they're not ideas we come across in the rest of our world – like how God can be everywhere and know everything that ever happened, or will happen, all at once! The Bible says that God is much bigger and more complicated than humans, so I believe that we can know God closely, but some things might stay mysterious until we meet Him face to face. That doesn't mean these things we learn about God aren't true, just that there is much more to discover!

Q57

d the
racles in
e Bible
lly happen?
miracles
ppen today?

Elspeth Darley,
chologist and
ologian

The Bible records over 100 miracles, like Moses splitting the sea in two, Jesus making blind people see, or the sky turning dark when He died. Even ancient non-Christian writers who knew Jesus said that He had "magical powers" to heal people and do "amazing deeds". Some people say a miracle is when something extraordinary happens that cannot be explained by science. And I think these kinds of miracles have happened and do still happen. These might involve God creating or healing something in a way that can't be explained with science – something outside of the way the universe normally works (see Q 53). The biggest example of this kind of miracle is Jesus rising from the dead and I definitely believe that happened.

I believe God can and does use science to do the extraordinary too. So, even if some miracles happen within nature, in ways that can be explained with science (like the eclipse of the sun or strong winds blowing the sea apart), then we can still think about them as miraculous. I think the important thing to remember is that the Bible calls miracles "signs" because they are always there to point us to God, who I believe is behind the things we can explain with science as well as those we can't.

Was the resurrection a trick?

Dr Matt Pritchard,
Physicist and
Magician

As a magician I spend lots of time thinking about how tricks work and how to make tricks happen. And lots of things make me think the resurrection couldn't have been a trick. One thing is that Roman soldiers had to be really good at their jobs. If a prisoner escaped, the guarding soldiers would be killed! So I don't think that when given the job to kill Jesus, they would let Him escape or let His death be faked. They would have made 100 per cent sure He was dead before His body was buried. Looking at all the eyewitness accounts and other evidence from the resurrection I think it is almost impossible to come up with any explanation other than Jesus really did die and come back to life! That almost sounds too good to be true, but I think that is the point! The Bible says if Jesus' resurrection didn't happen, the hope of the Christian faith vanishes and all that is left are stories about how to live a "good" life. Christians believe Jesus died and came back to life to show once and for all that the God who created everything has power over death, and to give people a way to live close to Him forever. This amazing claim certainly grabs people's attention – and for me, I am convinced it really happened.

Q59

God just an
swer for
ings science
n't help us
understand
t?

Hannah
nshaw,
ronomer

There are plenty of exciting mysteries we can't yet explain with science, but even if someday we can, God will still play a part in how I understand them. In my scientific field, we are learning about black holes and how they work. The more we discover, the more I ask myself: what might black holes tell me about God? Why might God create places where something can seem to disappear from the rest of the universe with no return? I am still thinking! New scientific discoveries don't replace God or make me doubt my faith but they can add to my thoughts about God.

I also think there are things that science will never fully help us understand. We could know everything about the stars, but that wouldn't tell me my purpose in the world. We could know everything about how to take care of nature, but we would still need to decide if we wanted to look after it. Knowing about how the world works doesn't tell us what is morally right or wrong. For me, learning about God helps me with these questions – science can contribute to how I think about them, but I will always need more than science to explore them fully.

Do our ideas about God change as we discover more science?

Prof. Tom McLeish,
Theoretical Physicist

Many of the people I believe God used to write the Bible say that God sometimes teaches us about Himself by inviting us to investigate the natural world. God reminds a man called Job to look at the world He has created to help Job understand that storms can help life flourish. Another man called Paul talks about the importance of learning through noticing creation, saying God's power is clear from "all that is made".

So it seems the Bible itself expects people to change their ideas about everything, including God, by learning about nature – the activity we now call "science". Science doesn't prove God's existence, but I think there are lots of exciting examples of how it helps us understand things about Him. The immense age of the universe teaches us about God's patience. The huge number of planets, stars, and galaxies, and the incredible diversity of life on Earth teach us about God's creativity. And studying climate science reminds us of the truth of God's warnings that our behaviour can have seriously destructive effects or impact the world for good.

Q61

'hat happens
hen we pray?

e Revd Prof.
avid Wilkinson,
trophysicist and
eologian

I believe God loves us so much He wants to always be in communication with us. Those of us who pray take part in that conversation. Sometimes we talk, thanking God for His gifts, or saying sorry for not living the kind of life He wants for us. Sometimes we listen and find out more about Him and His plans. We might not always hear a voice but I think God can also talk to people through parts of the Bible or things like words from a friend or a feeling in our hearts.

We can also ask God to help us and to do things like heal those who are sick. I think God likes us to ask for things, and He always answers our prayers, just not always with the answer we would expect! He might use one of His ways of talking to tell us "yes", "no", or "wait" depending on what He knows will be best for us in the long term.

Some people worry that the things we have learned through science tell us the future can't be changed, and so it's pointless asking God to do things. Interestingly, that doesn't seem to be what science says at all – scientific ideas called quantum and chaos theory actually show that the universe is not completely predictable. Either way, many Christians believe that God works both through and beyond the laws of physics to answer prayers.

Q62

Is religion just a crutch for people who can't cope with life?

Prof. Justin L. Barrett,
Developmental Psychologist

The Revd Dr Gillian Straine,
Physicist and Theologian

Religions can give us tools for making sense of our lives and many people find God a source of purpose and joy. But that doesn't mean religion isn't real. After all, when we are hungry, we don't imagine we are full to cope with it. And we don't invent gods just to feel better. In fact, some religious ideas are not comforting at all! For example, Christianity teaches that we should expect to face struggles. That doesn't seem very encouraging! Religion may help us in our struggles but it is about much more than that.

If a crutch is real, it can really help! There is no one who is able to cope with life all of the time – everyone will struggle at some point in their life. We should never feel embarrassed or scared to ask for help. So what is wrong with having a crutch? Sometimes, it is when we struggle, ask for help, and perhaps even pray to God that we discover how much friends, family, and God care about us and give us the strength and courage to keep going.

Q63

e there
y extinct
igions?

k Spencer,
orian of Ideas

Probably! Most people who have ever lived, and languages that have ever been spoken, are no longer with us. It is probably the same with religions. Today we think about "religion" quite differently from how people have through most of history. But most (perhaps all) cultures in history seem to have had beliefs in the spirit world, patterns of worship, rituals, and ethical codes of the sort that could be called "religion".

Archaeology shows signs of prehistoric religious practice like ritual burial or stone circles. Ancient texts and monuments reveal religions, such as those of the Ancient Egyptians, or the Druids of Britain. And there are more recent examples. When the Spanish first sailed to Central America in the sixteenth century, they encountered interesting religions which are now extinct. So it seems there have been lots of different ways of "doing religion" throughout history, and it's been an important part of most or all cultures. There are lots of fascinating questions to ask about this, like: what draws people to ask religious questions, and which ideas about God or gods have stood the test of time, and why?

If people have created religion, does that mean God doesn't exist?

Dr Emily Burdett,
Developmental Psychologist

Absolutely not! Just think about this for a moment. If God does exist, wouldn't it make sense that the people He created would find ways to learn about and worship Him? I think religious practices such as rituals, prayers, songs, and special holidays are things humans have come up with to try and explore our Big Questions, and to help us get to know God in unique and powerful ways. Although these practices were created by humans, I think they serve to honour, praise, and communicate with God.

But there are lots of different ideas about God so it's important for us to explore which claims we think are true and important. For example, Christianity claims there is one God who made everything and loves us so much that He came to Earth as a human, lived, died, and came back to life to make that possible! To decide what we think is true, we can look at the historical reliability of religious texts, the way they have changed over time and the way people's lives are changed by their religious faith (see Q 94). What we decide might change the way we live!

Q65

w would
e world be
ferent if
ere was no
ligion?

k Spencer,
torian of Ideas

f there was no religion in the world, humans would probably invent one! In fact, that is precisely what we've done, many times. Several societies have tried to erase religion altogether, but the result wasn't a lack of religion. Some people continued to hold on to religions they believed were true and important, and other people created new ones! Even when people didn't worship a god, they seemed to end up worshipping "cleverness", "humanity", "money", "beauty", the "self" or the "great leader". It seems humans need to worship something, whether an idea, an aim in life, or a god. It is interesting to ask why we're like this, but the choice isn't as simple as religion or no religion; it's more about what we think is worth worshipping.

Emily Burdett,
velopmental
chologist

I am not sure the world could ever have no religion. Throughout history and all over the world we've seen how religion inspires people to act, providing meaning, morals, and a social network. In some areas of the world (like Scandinavia), we see that religion is no longer common. These areas are in a state of peace and their governments provide good quality health care, social and mental welfare, high wages, and good living and working conditions, so it might seem there's less need for some of what religion often supplies. But some religion still exists in these places and there are lots of questions to ask about whether we can satisfy all our Big Questions without ideas about God.

CHAPTER 6

Wonderful World

Questions About Life on Earth

GETTING STARTED:

Why do we ask questions?

Prof. Justin L. Barrett,
Developmental Psychologist

We aren't strong like buffalos, fast like zebras, agile like leopards or tough and fierce like wolverines. Yet, humans have spread into every corner of the world and even spent time in space. I think one secret to our success is our ability to learn from our surroundings and each other. Little children, especially, drive their parents crazy by asking "why?". And why not? Curiosity is how we explore questions, develop new ideas, solve problems, gather knowledge, and share it with others.

Some scientists think the human brain evolved to become so big (compared to our body size) because gradual brain size increases allowed our ancestors to better learn together and share knowledge. Isn't it great that we don't have to spend our time trying to figure everything out on our own! Instead, we can use our time and curiosity to learn from others, add improvements to old ideas and come up with new ones.

Another reason we ask questions is to connect with each other. Humans are unusually social animals. We spend lots of time interacting and forming deep relationships. We care about family. We make friends. We ask about what they like and don't like, how they're feeling, what they plan to do tomorrow. Learning to understand and care for each other also helps us learn and solve problems together. So asking questions is an important part of being human!

GETTING PERSONAL:

What is your favourite part of working in science?

Cara Parrett,
Marine Biologist

I love learning how things work, then going out into the world and seeing them in action. There is pure beauty in the world which we can all enjoy, but I feel that science reveals secret little wonders that make me smile even wider. I can lie in my garden and just enjoy clouds because, "Hey, that one looks like a dragon", or huddle up inside with hot chocolate during a hailstorm enjoying the colour of the sky. But I can also use what I know from science to imagine each tiny water droplet zooming around, bumping into others, being blown up through the middle of the cloud, high into the sky, freezing, and falling back towards the ground where I sit watching. Amazing!

Snorkelling with sea turtles in the Maldives I knew the male turtle became a "he" because his egg was slightly cooler in its sandy nest than those which became females. When I saw turtle mothers crawling up the beach to lay eggs, I knew they had travelled the oceans for years, until it was time to lay their eggs, then they swam straight back to the island where they were born 30 years before!

Science is about asking questions and unlocking treasure-troves of hidden gems. As a Christian, I believe God made and loves everything, so science also inspires me to praise and worship God! I hope you can go out into the world, explore, enjoy, wonder, and maybe worship too!

Q66

How old is the earth? What was it like at the beginning?

Prof. Bob White,
Geophysicist

Science tells us Earth is about 4,567 million (4,567,000,000) years old (to remember, say "4-5-6-7-million"). That might seem old but Earth is actually quite young. The universe is three times older! Like other planets, Earth was made from dust and bits of rock from old stars which exploded into millions of tiny pieces. Some of those bits clumped together to make our sun, the earth and the other planets in our solar system.

Early on, Earth was very hot, mostly melted, and there were many volcanoes. There were no plants or animals, no air to breathe, and no oceans or lakes. For a long time, Earth was being hit by lots of massive meteorites which made enormous craters like those on the moon. Eventually Earth cooled down and the rocky surface became hard. Oceans, lakes, and rivers started to form, and life began (see Q 67)! After thousands of millions of years of evolution, plants, animals, and then, even later, people lived all over Earth.

Q67

When did life begin?

Prof. Hugh Rollinson,
Geochemist

The oldest life we know of is from about 3,700 million (3,700,000,000) years ago and scientists think life began just before that. When Earth first formed, life probably could not have survived (see Q 66). But once Earth became calmer it seems life appeared very quickly.

The earliest fossils of living things we have found are from ancient rocks in Greenland. They are just tiny black blobs in the rock and don't look very interesting! But we can tell they were once alive by using complex scientific equipment to study the chemicals in these fossils. These early creatures were probably each made of just one cell, and the same was true of most living things for over 3,000 million years. But they were gradually evolving. And from about 540 million years ago lots and lots of more complex (multi-celled) fossils are found. This change could mean there was a sudden "explosion" of evolution into different life forms, or maybe the fossils don't yet give us the full picture, but that's another exciting question! As a Christian, I believe God creates life and I love exploring these questions about how He does it.

Q68

at came
st: the
icken or
e egg?

April Maskiewicz
dero,
ogist

The answer is reptiles! Huh? Well, you see, eggs have been around for a long time and *many* different types of female animals produce eggs, including female humans! So there are actually lots of ways to answer this question, but let me explain why reptiles is a good answer. For some animals, including humans and most other mammals, the egg grows and develops inside the female until she gives birth to the baby animal. Other animals lay their eggs and the baby grows in the egg until it is big enough to hatch out. The eggs of fish and amphibians (like frogs and salamanders) do not have a thick hard shell so they have to lay their eggs in wet environments to stop them drying out. But around 300 million years ago, reptiles (like snakes and turtles) were the first group of animals that evolved to lay eggs with hard shells. The hard shell stops the egg drying out and allows animals to reproduce on land instead of near water. Birds evolved much later (as part of a group of dinosaurs!) and can lay their eggs in even drier environments because of the yolk that breaks down to provide water for the developing chick. So next time you are eating an egg, thank a reptile!

Q69

Why did God make so many different types of animals and plants?

Dr Sarah Bodbyl Roels,
Evolutionary Biologist

I don't think any of us fully understand this. But it is exciting to think about! The Bible tells us creation is a way God pours out His amazing love and that He takes great delight in it. I also think God often seems to enjoy slowly unfolding His plans – bringing things into being through processes which give them time and opportunity to change and flourish. So perhaps it is enough to think that God made so many different things purely because He enjoys them and loves creating.

The Bible also says we can learn about God through creation. We can stare in wonder at the amazing shapes and colours of orchids, hummingbirds, and elephants, or marvel at the intricate processes which drive this diversity. I think the wonderful variety we see tells us about a God who has a vastly creative imagination and who delights in beauty and diversity. I think God loves it when we discover and enjoy His creation and learn more about Him from it.

Q70

Why are there so many stories about dragons, unicorns, and other imaginary creatures?

Prof. Cara Wall-Scheffler, Anthropologist

All human populations seem to have stories about mythical creatures such as dragons, sea monsters, or cyclops. Humans are really good at imagining and we think these myths mostly came from a mixture of imagination with wonder about real life creatures. Interesting living things like elephants and giraffes, and fossils of unfamiliar animals that we now know were things like dinosaurs or ichthyosaurs, all seem to have inspired parts of these imaginary creatures. Many had added details like wings, magical powers, or underground lairs and some, like mermaids, were even made of different creatures mixed together. One of the world's oldest sculptures is a human with the head of a lion!

Ideas about mythical creatures actually show us something very important about how humans not only observe the world around us but use imagination to explore ideas beyond the limits of what we see. This might mean imagining enormous dragons or tiny human-like fairies, but it is also important for considering real things like countries we've never visited, particles too small to see, or the enormous size of the universe. This ability to think beyond what we see is also important for helping us understand ideas about God.

How did the dinosaurs die out? What would life be like if they hadn't?

Prof. Mary Higby Schweitzer,
Palaeontologist

Dinosaurs didn't die out! They are alive and well, as colourful feathered friends in your garden. Just like chihuahuas are a type of dog, birds are a type of dinosaur. Imagine if all dogs except chihuahuas were extinct. Wouldn't that change your idea of what dogs look like?

But what happened to the "non-avian" (non-bird) dinosaurs? This is one of the exciting mysteries of the past and we have discovered lots but we still don't know for sure. Dinosaurs lived on Earth a very long time (far longer than humans have) and lots of different groups of them came and went during that time. But a big mass extinction about 66 million years ago took out all the dinosaurs, except birds. Our best idea about what happened is that many different things added up. A big meteorite impact and global climate change probably played a part. Also, major land masses that had been isolated for a long time were gradually becoming linked, allowing dinosaurs to come into new contact with each other, perhaps spreading diseases.

An even more interesting question to me is why birds survived and why they are still very successful. Was it because they were smaller, more warm-blooded, or able to fly? We don't know everything, but we're working on some exciting research!

Q72

hat is
e most
dangered
imal in the
orld?

ra Parrett,
rine Biologist

It can be hard to count wild animals. Imagine trying to count seahorses who are good at hiding, or mole rats who live underground. We don't actually know how many species there are, let alone how each kind is doing! Now imagine trying to count animals when there aren't many left. Tricky!

Scientists are trying to monitor the very endangered animals we know about. Hidden cameras watch for the 70-90 Amur leopards left in Russia and China, endangered because of hunting and deforestation. Underwater microphones listen for the 22 remaining dolphin-like vaquitas near Mexico, endangered by fishing. Other animals are only left in zoos, like the three Yangtze giant softshell turtles left in the world. And there could be other animals in danger that we haven't even discovered yet. Human activities threaten many animals, but we are also working hard to save species from extinction - it can and does happen. When humans are the threat, we can also be the solution if we work together to care well for creation.

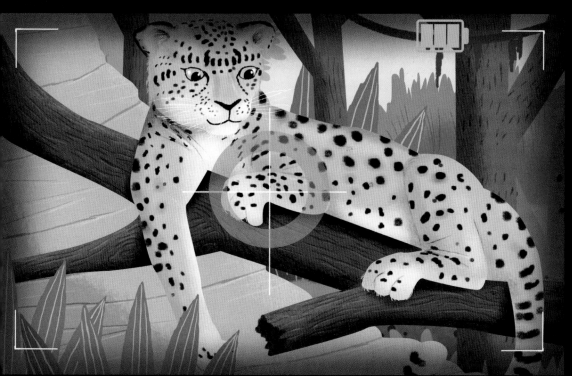

Q73

Does God have a favourite animal?

Dr Margaret W. Miller,
Marine Ecologist

Favourites are tricky! Do you have more than one favourite colour, or favourite food? Can you choose easily between pizza or brownies? The Bible says God created all the different kinds of animals, along with the earth and all the natural systems that sustain them such as water, sunlight, nutrients, and plants. The first story in the Bible says God demonstrated His love for *all* the animals He made by declaring that they were "good" and blessing them. Another story in the Bible is about God providing an ark, and a caretaker named Noah, to rescue animals from a massive flood (see Q 88). It says God then made a special promise with *every* type of animal. So I think it's pretty clear that God loves everything He's made and doesn't have favourites! Even so, the Bible tells us God does have a special relationship with one type of animal that He chose to make "in His own image" – humans (see Q 44)!

Q74

Are there any undiscovered animals?

Dr Nick Higgs,
Marine Biologist

Yes! We still discover new species every year. So far, scientists have discovered more than 1.5 million species of animals, and we think we've probably found most of the big, obvious ones, as well as lots and lots of smaller ones! A quarter of all known living species are beetles (there's even a running joke among scientists that God must have a special fondness for beetles). Another quarter of known species live in the oceans, but we know there is much more to discover in their depths. On a recent expedition we found a new kind of pill bug (woodlouse) the size of a human thumb, living in the deep sea.

The best guess scientists have for the total number of animal species alive today is about 8 million, and that's just animals that exist today. Millions of species have gone extinct over Earth's long history and some of these are still being discovered as fossils. So yes! There is a lot left to find, and each new discovery tells us more about the wonderful world we are part of. Perhaps one day you'll discover a new type of animal?

Q75

umans didn't st, would ather animal ve taken over e we have?

f. Simon way Morris, ogist

Scientists often wonder what might have happened if evolution had taken different paths. Would an alternative evolutionary history without whales, daisies, hippos, or lettuces make much difference? What about no humans? It might seem like a strange world, but maybe it wouldn't be all that different. When we look at evolution we see the same solutions being developed over and over again. This is called convergent evolution, and it is part of our history too. For example, our eyes are remarkably similar to those of an octopus, even though we are only very distant relatives. Other animals have developed very similarly to us in our ability to pick up and move objects precisely, use tools, or walk on two legs. We are also not alone in evolving large brains and advanced intelligence.

We do show some odd features that seem to have allowed us to "take over" in some ways. Other animals communicate, but no others have language (see Q 76). Some use tools, but don't use one tool to make another like we do. Many people think our language and technology allow us to do, think, imagine, and discover things that no other animal can. So it is not impossible that another animal could have ended up a lot like us, and if we ever meet creatures from another planet, I wouldn't be too surprised if they were quite a bit like us.

Do any other animals talk like us?

Dr David Lahti,
Behavioural Biologist

Many species of animals communicate using sounds. Some use their mouths, others use legs, wings or other body parts. Most develop these sounds automatically (like babies knowing how to cry). But whales and dolphins, some bats, and many birds, actually learn their sounds from parents and other elders. If they were raised alone, they would never learn their species' sounds.

Humans learn like this too, but there is a big difference. When other animals "speak", they mainly seem to talk about themselves and their immediate needs or feelings - "Here I am!", "I am hungry!", "Here is food!", "Danger is coming!", "Get away from me!", or "Come here!". But humans use sounds to represent our world in much more specific ways - "red" means a particular colour, and "ball" means a spherical object. On top of that, we put words together to describe ideas or feelings like beauty, hope, and love. This "symbolic" language is special and seems to be uniquely human.

Q77

Do any other animals have religion?

Dr Emily Burdett,
Developmental
Psychologist

Some people think that some animals show signs of religion. Elephants have been known to bury dead elephants and even other dead animals they encounter. And there are videos of wild chimpanzees throwing and piling rocks next to a tree. This is fascinating because there is no apparent purpose to their behaviour so it's possible that the piling of rocks is a ritual. But it's a long way from human religion today and it's not enough to convince us that animals have religion.

David Lahti,
Behavioural Biologist

It's very difficult to tell what's going on inside the heads of other animals. We think some animals experience relationships and emotions on deep levels that might be similar to parts of human religious experiences. But we don't think any other animals are capable of thinking about life after death, whether God exists, or their relationship with God. Humans seem to have evolved abilities to question, wonder, and communicate in unique ways that made religion possible. Religion then became an important part of every human society and culture.

Q78

Is beauty in nature important? If so, why did God make it?

Prof. Jeff Hardin,
Developmental
Biologist

Beauty is definitely important in nature. Generally speaking, different species are attracted to very different features. Male proboscis monkeys with especially big noses are attractive to female proboscis monkeys, but they wouldn't win any human beauty contests! This kind of "beauty" is very important for helping animals find the most successful mates. But humans see beauty in other things too. We might see beauty in a sunset or a peacock's tail. And some people find beauty in maths. To you an equation might just be a puzzle in an exam. But when scientists find a simple equation that describes something really important (like how light or gravity works) they often call that "beautiful".

Why do we find these sorts of things beautiful? The Bible teaches that an incredibly inventive, loving God created the whole universe, and that He delights in it all, from intricate flowers and wild animals, to the sun and stars. Christians believe that God finds His creation beautiful and made us able to discover and enjoy it with Him. I think that's part of the adventure of science – experiencing and discovering the beauty in God's creation.

CHAPTER 7

Good God? Bad God?

Questions About What God is Like

No! As a scientist, doubt is a key tool because it helps me ask great questions, test theories, and explore this extraordinary world. Doubt drives scientists to keep questioning and exploring new ideas, correcting, or improving theories, never settling or stopping learning about the universe. There is always more to know, and that is exciting. One of my heroes, Richard Feynman, said: "Nobody ever figures out what life is all about, and it doesn't matter. Explore the world. Nearly everything is really interesting if you go into it deeply enough."

As a Christian, doubt is also important! There are many streams of knowledge that flow into Christian faith. The Bible, the tradition of the church, and even our personal experiences of things like prayer can all help us feel confident about our faith. But sometimes things happen that make us doubt – someone might get ill, or our prayers might not seem to be getting an answer. Many great people of faith in the Bible had doubts and questions too! Like with science, exploring our questions can strengthen our ideas and understanding. Christianity is not about having all the answers to all the questions; it is about asking questions honestly and believing that God loves us, whatever is happening around us.

GETTING
PERSONAL:

What are
the biggest
challenges
you've faced in
your scientific
career?

Prof. John Wyatt,
Medical Doctor
& Ethicist

One of my biggest challenges came when I was working as a doctor caring for very sick babies and as a scientific researcher trying to find ways of reducing brain damage in newborn babies after a difficult birth. Our laboratory experiments (not using people) showed that cooling could reduce the amount of brain damage. But nobody knew whether it would be safe to cool a newborn human baby. In fact, textbooks for doctors said babies should always be kept warm!

I had to decide whether it would be OK to organize an experiment (called a clinical trial) with real human babies to test our new cooling treatment. After months of discussion with other scientists, doctors, and ethics experts, we decided to start the experiment. We studied 230 babies around the world who were at high risk of brain damage or death. Their parents all agreed for their babies to be part of the experiment because they hoped the cooling treatment would help.

With scientific research you never know what the outcome will be and I was very nervous that things would go badly. To my relief, our risk paid off: the experiment showed that babies who received the treatment were more likely to survive without any damage compared with babies who didn't get the treatment. Cooling treatment is now used in hospitals around the world – even the textbooks have changed!

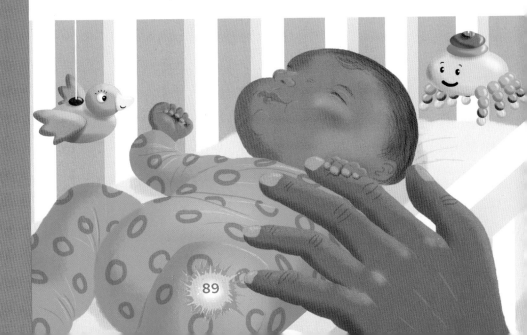

**Who is God?
What does
God look like?**

The Right Revd
Prof. Dr N. T.
Wright,
New Testament
Scholar

The Bible is pretty clear that we can't see God most of the time, and it talks about Him being mysterious in some ways. Different parts of the Bible use all sorts of different pictures to try to describe who He is. This seems to show that He's just too big and amazing to get our minds around! But that doesn't mean we shouldn't try to learn more about Him. I believe that the best ideas we have of what God is like come from Jesus. Jesus is described as God in human form. This means that we can look at Jesus to see who God is. The Bible tells us that Jesus was loving, kind, and powerful. For example, He shocked people by showing love to those who were outcasts, unloved by or unimportant to others. Lots of the things that Jesus did can help us to see how much God loves each one of us, and everything else He has made. This is one of the most important parts of who God is.

In science we use the word "random" to mean that we cannot predict everything about an event. For example, we cannot predict the precise speed of each particular air molecule in a room. But if we know the room temperature, we can predict the average speed of the air molecules and we can do a lot with that! To make sense of the random event we need to look at the bigger picture. Like with "random" events in science, sometimes in life, looking at the big picture can help us make more sense of events that we don't understand at the time.

Life can seem like a series of disconnected happenings. But I believe that everything has a cause. It might be down to poverty, or ideas, or individuals. Even if it's not to do with humans, maybe it's something to do with the planet's natural processes. We can't control much. But we can control how we react to events. If we respond to our mixed-up world with love and openness and imagination, we will make the best of every situation.

If you're standing right next to a painting, it can look like just a random bunch of colours and patterns. In a similar way, our lives, or even the world, can sometimes look totally random and out of control. However, I believe God is creating a masterpiece with His plans for the world, including you and me! We might not be able to see it from where we are now, but we can trust God is a master painter.

Q81

Does the Bible say there was no death when God first made the world?

Dr Bethany Sollereder,
Theologian

The Bible creation stories tell us God made everything "good" (or "fit for purpose"). But we don't think of death as "good", so people wonder whether God intended it. We know there was some death in the creation story because God commanded creatures to eat – carrots, grass, and pomegranates have to die to be eaten! And science shows us that many basic processes of life require physical death: even cells in our bodies have to die so we can grow properly and stay healthy. Many great Christian thinkers, like Augustine and Aquinas, have said that these kinds of physical death have always been part of God's good world. Others, like Martin Luther, have disagreed.

What most Christian thinkers do agree on is that the Bible says there is a kind of death that comes from the broken relationship between people, God, and the world (see Q 23). I think this kind of "spiritual death", or separation from the way God made us to be, is a big part of what makes some kinds of physical death so sad. But the Bible also says that that separation from God is what Jesus came to heal and restore. I believe that through the power of Jesus' own death and resurrection, God heals that separation, and that one day the sadness of death will end in the new life God promises in the Bible (see Q 10).

Q82

y did
d choose
create
ough
lution
ich involves
much death
d suffering?

Denis Alexander,
chemist

I think evolution is a wonderful process through which God has been using tiny changes in each generation to fill His world with a beautiful variety of living things over billions of years. But it seems to require pain (see Q 84) and death (see Q 81). Apart from most plants, almost all living things eat others. And if nothing ever died, there wouldn't be space or materials for new generations to grow and develop. The Bible says there are some things we can't yet understand about God. I think this question might be one of them. But that doesn't mean we shouldn't explore it.

The Bible says that God is good and loves all He has made, that God understands much more about life and death than we do, and that His power over it extends beyond our universe (see Q 90 and Chapter 8 "Getting Started"). It also tells us God understands pain and suffering – saying God came to Earth, as Jesus, and suffered pain, loss, sadness, and even death. So, for Christians, even though we may never understand why there is pain, death or suffering in our world, we can be sure that God understands, wants to help us explore our Big Questions, and that His love for all of His creation is bigger than we could ever imagine.

If God is really in control, why are there so many natural disasters?

The Revd Dr Roger P. Abbott,
Practical Theologian

I t is always upsetting to hear about natural disasters and the people who suffer or die because of them. But science shows that earthquakes, volcanoes, storms, floods, and wildfires each have special ways of helping keep our planet healthy – for example, volcanoes make soil better for growing plants. And the Bible includes songs written by people thinking about these events and praising God's power as creator.

So if they can be good, why do these awe-inspiring natural events sometimes cause problems? I think the problems start when people make bad choices about how we treat the natural world. For example, to save money people might choose to use cheap materials to build weak houses, so when earthquakes happen people can get hurt or tragically die. The extra sad thing is that it's often richer people who make choices that lead to poorer people (who have no choice) getting hurt. I believe God has made an incredible world and given humans a big responsibility to protect people and the planet. But He also shares His wisdom for how to live well and gives us the creativity and intelligence to put it into action. I think if we do this more, we'll see things get much better.

Q84

uld God
e created
niverse
ere there
s no
fering?

Michael J.
ray,
osopher

Suffering happens when we have bad feelings, like physical or emotional pain. So one way God could create a world without suffering would be to make a world filled with only robots that have no feelings at all. But feelings are good! The most meaningful things in our lives - being creative, having friends, and loving each other or God - involve feelings. I believe God made us to be people who experience feelings. But couldn't God have created a universe where we have only good feelings? Unfortunately, I can't really see how that would work in our world - good and bad feelings seem to be closely linked and important for us. For example, science shows having an "alarm system" that lets us know when we're in danger keeps our bodies safe from serious injury - pain is a very effective alarm system. And painful emotions seem to be very closely linked to happy ones. When we enjoy being with our friends, or love someone, we experience powerful, good emotions of happiness and joy. But this means that when we lose friends or people we love, our happiness and joy can also be taken away, causing sadness and distress.

We may never understand exactly why suffering exists in our universe. But as a Christian, I find it important to remember that the Bible says God understands (see Q 82). It says we can choose to one day live with God in a "new creation" where, somehow, suffering will end even though we are still exactly as God made us to be (see Q 10).

Do I make decisions about my life or does God control everything I do?

Prof. Tim O'Connor,
Philosopher

To explore this question, I think about two important ways I believe God relates to us: He creates us, and He wants to be our friend. You could build a robot that is programmed to act like your friend, but that wouldn't be real friendship. And some people truly are our friends, but we didn't create them. To create us so we could be His friends, I think God had to do something special – make us able to make our own choices. We can choose many things, but some are outside our control. Things like where we are born or who our parents are can affect our opportunities and the way we live. These things are often more about other people's choices than ours.

But I believe God creates the entire universe, everywhere we might go and everyone whose choices might affect us. So my best answer is: God is in control of the big picture of my life and everyone else's, but He invites me to choose how to respond to lots of life's situations and opportunities. Because I believe God wants to be our friend and knows what's best for us, I think if we ask Him, He will always help us make good choices or face difficult circumstances.

at's the
nt of
ng good?

Roger
therton,
hologist

When I was a kid and going to a friend's house, my parents would say, "Be good." They meant that I should say "please" and "thank you", be kind, share sensibly, avoid mischief, and try not to break anything. Little did they know I would grow up to be a psychologist who studies being grateful, kind, careful, and fair! Psychologists call these "character strengths", and these ideas of who we are when we are at our best have been studied for decades.

We have found that being good is actually good for us! Being grateful, loving, kind, and so on, is not just a nice way to be. People like that are often happier, healthier, enjoy being around others, feel life is worth living, and can even do better in school. This makes lots of sense. It doesn't always work this way, but generally, if you are kind to others they are kind to you and if you tell the truth, other people tell you the truth. I think an amazing example of this is where the Bible says we can love God, people, and our world really well because of how much God loves each one of us.

Where does anger come from?

The Revd Dr Joanna Collicutt, Neuropsychologist and Theologian

Lots of things can make us feel angry. Often, we feel anger when we think a rule has been broken. (How many times have you yelled "It's not fair!"?) Being angry can sometimes be good! It helps us to protect ourselves or others from bad situations. The Bible says that Jesus got angry like this when He saw weak or poor people being hurt. Like Jesus, anger might make us want to change things for the better – to sign a petition or collect money to give to someone who needs help. Sometimes we get angry when something unfair happens to somebody we love – maybe they're being bullied, they get sick, or perhaps they even die. Feeling angry (including feeling angry with God) is a natural part of that sadness. Quite a lot of the Bible is written by people who are angry and sad about situations like that and trying to make sense of things. But we don't need to stay angry forever. Talking honestly to friends can help a lot. I think we can talk to God too, even praying angry prayers. Doctors and counsellors can also help if we ever get stuck with angry feelings or get angry in a way that hurts or frightens ourselves or others. We might still feel some sadness, and we can still act to make things better, but talking to God and people can help our anger to pass in time.

We sometimes have to do things we wish we didn't. Police put criminals in jail, not because they want to but because there's no other way to keep others safe. The Bible story about the flood talks about humans doing such terrible, violent, scary things that God had to act. He got His faithful friend Noah to warn people and waited patiently for them to change, but finally He chose to end the chaos. The Bible talks about the flood being like God "uncreating" the world to start again. It might be talking about a flood covering the whole earth, or just Noah's local area, or it might be just a story. But part of its message is about people and animals dying as punishment for the bad choices people made, and that can be upsetting to think about. But the story says God took care to rescue Noah's family and the animals that needed protecting, and it finishes with God making a promise that nothing like that will happen again. I think Jesus' death and resurrection gives a glimpse of God's plan to keep this promise and make everything right, not just for humans, but the whole of His creation (see Chapter 8 "Getting Started").

The Bible says God asks us to love one another. We especially find this in Jesus' teachings, where He tells us the best way to live is to be kind, respect others, be truthful, and live peacefully together. But it's not always easy to do that, is it? Sometimes we make good choices and love people well like Jesus said, but sometimes we make bad choices, and then we sometimes do things that hurt people. It might seem simpler for God to stop us hurting others but the Bible says God doesn't force us to live the right way. It teaches that, because He loves us, God wants us to choose to love Him back and care for other people. So He has created us with the freedom and ability to choose what to do and how to act. That's a lot of responsibility! But I believe God understands and forgives us when we mess up and always wants to help us! I believe that with the Bible's teaching and with God as our friend, we can get better at making wise and loving choices.

The Revd Dr Rodney Holder,
Cosmologist and Theologian

Prof. John Wyatt,
Medical Doctor and Ethicist

Yes, I believe that when we die, we go to be with God forever. I believe this because I trust the evidence that Jesus rose from the dead. The writers of the Bible's New Testament either saw Jesus alive again themselves or knew and trusted others who had seen Him alive again. The Bible tells us Jesus promised eternal life after death to anyone who believes in Him and I am convinced that there are many good reasons to believe this is true.

Science cannot answer this question because when we talk about life after death, we usually mean that "something else" of a person, a "soul" or "spirit", continues after death. But it's not possible to use scientific instruments to detect whether a person continues to exist in some form after the death of our body on Earth. Some scientists believe that all the information which describes a person could be recorded and saved in a different form, a bit like uploading a file to "the cloud". But for me, this form of digital "life" after death is very different from the astonishing claims of the Christian faith that I find very compelling. I believe Jesus defeated death and therefore after our own death we will be raised physically as part of a new creation.

CHAPTER 8

Friends or Foes?

Questions About Science and Religious Faith

ETTING
ARTED:

here is
aven?
at is it like?

Revd Prof.
id Wilkinson,
rophysicist and
ologian

The word "heaven" is used by Christians to mean different things but we often mean "where we go to live with God after we die". We sometimes think about heaven being somehow "up in the sky" with angelic people sitting around on clouds. But (thankfully!) what Christians believe the Bible teaches is much more exciting than that! The Bible says that when people die believing in Jesus they are given a new body and will go to a new heaven and earth, a transformed version of this world, which will be like this world, but unimaginably better and free from any suffering.

As far as we can tell, the "new creation" the Bible talks about isn't part of the universe as we know it. Which means it is hard to describe or understand where it is. Science helps us understand that everything we do, measure, and describe in our universe exists in "space-time". That's three dimensions of space (up/down, left/right, and forward/backward), and one of time. So if heaven isn't part of this universe, and doesn't exist within our space-time, I just don't think we have the language or ability to understand where it is.

But just because humans can't understand it yet doesn't mean that heaven isn't real. In the Bible, Jesus used lots of pictures to explain important things about how He would make a way for us to join Him in heaven. And I believe that when He came back to life, Jesus showed us that His (and the Bible's) teaching about life after death, including heaven, can be trusted.

GETTING
PERSONAL:

Would 10-year-
old you be
surprised by
what you've
done with
your life so far?

Dr Denis Alexander,
Biochemist

Yes, my 10-year-old self would be really surprised by some things, but not everything that has happened. My mother was a scientist, so I got plenty of my love for science from her. My grandfather was a doctor. He died in the First World War, so I never knew him. But my father inherited his microscope which I used to look at little wriggly things from the garden. Fascinating. So no big surprise that I became a scientist!

The more surprising bit of life was that I became a follower of Christ when I was 13. That changed the direction of my life a lot. One thing Jesus said really challenged me – if you've been given much, then much more is expected from you. I'd been given much: loving parents, good education, wonderful science – so I ended up deciding to spend 15 years in the Middle East helping with science education. For five years I worked in a hospital in the middle of a civil war. Sheltering in a corridor with shooting all around and my children curled up beside me – that wasn't how 10-year-old me had imagined life! Following Christ can lead to surprises. It's not always easy but I would choose life with God any day!

Q91

hat is
ience?
pes everyone
gree?

of. Hasok Chang,
losopher

Science is the human activity of trying to learn about nature in a precise and ordered way. People tend to respect "scientific" things – it's like a stamp of approval. So by "science" we really mean a *good* way of learning about nature. But not everyone agrees what that looks like, and different fields of science work differently (see Chapter 1 "Getting Started").

One general idea about how science works is that we learn from experience, from trying things out. We don't just believe what someone says, but check it out ourselves by observation and experiment. To do good science we don't start with our minds made up. Even if we think we know the answer, we need to be open to the possibility of new observations and experiments changing what we know. Some people talk about science proving things, but most scientists recognize that we never truly have absolute proofs in science. We just build up more evidence to improve our knowledge. I believe that science should be based on humility. Learning happens best when we are open and curious.

Q92

Are there any limits to what we can do with science?

Dr April Maskiewicz Cordero,
Biologist

Scientific research has given us many wonderful things, from healthcare and computers, to breathtaking images of our solar system. There are still lots of exciting mysteries that scientists are exploring. But science can only answer particular kinds of questions – questions about the physical processes or mechanisms of creation; the natural laws that govern our universe.

Other questions like, "Why are we here?", "What is our purpose?", and "What's the right thing to do?" are not fully answerable by science, but they are some of the most important questions we ask (see Q 59). Religious faith is a different way of exploring our existence. It's not as helpful for understanding the processes of how things work, but better for helping us explore Big Questions about things outside of nature, like making choices about what's important, right or wrong, and understanding our purpose.

Right Revd
. Dr N. T.
ght,
Testament
olar

I think "faith" is simply trusting something or someone – like trusting the rope when you're abseiling down a cliff, or trusting a friend who's leading you along a dark path that they know and you don't. For followers of Jesus, "faith" means trusting that when Jesus died and rose again, the one true and living God was acting in powerful love to rescue His whole creation, including humans.

Many people use the word "faith" in a more general sense, meaning any belief about God and the world. We might also call this "religious faith". What this kind of faith looks like depends on what people believe about God. If they think of God as distant and detached, their faith might be a bit detached from the way they live. I believe that God was personally present and lovingly active in Jesus, so my faith is a grateful response, flowing naturally into love for God, everything, and everyone He has made.

Spencer,
orian of Ideas

Today, the word "faith" is often used in the context of "faith groups" (also known as "religions"). But "faith" is also more generally taken to mean committing to something when we can't be 100 per cent sure it's true or reliable. That is actually the case with many of the decisions we make in life. We use this kind of faith all the time. Whether we are choosing our A-levels or university, where to live, who to marry, who to vote for, what job to do, or what we think about God, we use faith based on evidence from things, people, institutions, or simply our instincts. Indeed, even in science, we don't usually say we have 100 per cent "proof" of anything – and we often talk about "believing" in a hypothesis or the conclusions we draw from a particular experiment.

UNIVERSE

What evidence is there for God and faith?

Dr Althea Wilkinson, Astronomer

Exploring the universe was one of the things that first made me wonder about God. I don't think science can prove or disprove the existence of God because science is about studying the physical, natural universe, and a God who created the whole universe must somehow be "beyond" or "outside" it and therefore beyond the power of science to understand. But I do believe that science can show us evidence of how amazing a creator God must be and teach us something about Him. To me, the fact that there is anything at all, and that the universe appears to be ordered, and to operate according to rules we can study and understand, is evidence that God the creator is hugely powerful, imaginative, and full of love for life and us.

Francis S.
llins,
eticist

Science and maths are wonderful ways of exploring our amazing universe. And lots of people find that the more we discover about how incredible and unlikely the universe is, the more we wonder if there's an intelligence behind it all. But science and maths don't tell us everything. We need to look at other kinds of evidence to answer our questions about why there is something instead of nothing, what is the meaning of right or wrong, whether God exists, and what God is like.

We might explore evidence like reliable documents of Scripture or the lived experience of religious people throughout history. As you put these together, I believe you will discover that all aspects of life and the universe make much more sense if there is a God behind the universe, an author of creation who writes the whole book.

Revd Dr
ana Collicutt,
ropsychologist
Theologian

I think that Jesus is the best evidence there is for God. He is more special and surprising than anything you could make up. He showed us a totally different way of understanding the world, based on loving other people until it hurt, instead of trying to be top dog. Beginning with the first followers 2,000 years ago, people find that if they put their faith in Him, He turns up, lets them know they are loved, and helps them to live like He did.

**Can we trust
faith as much
as scientific
fact?**

Prof. Paul Fairchild,
Stem Cell Biologist

We need to think carefully about what we trust. It might seem easier to trust science than faith because we understand that science is based on observations and experiments. But I think we often misunderstand what "faith" really is. We actually all live by faith, even if we call it something different. When we "assume" that every time we turn the tap on, water will flow, it's because we have faith there will always be enough rainfall. We have faith in doctors to give us the right medicine when we're sick, and faith in that medicine to make us better. We even have faith that our science is telling us the truth about the world. So we often trust faith because it involves gathering evidence, often from past experiences, to help us make safe assumptions. My faith in God is also based on evidence like this and I believe it's worth trusting because He always wants the best for us.

Q96

ve science
d religious
th always
en at war?

f. John
lley Brooke,
torian of Science

No! Since scientific exploration of the universe began, there have been many conversations about how this fits with belief in God. But does belief in a creator God have to mean war with science? Certainly not. Many famous scientists have had religious faith. In the 1600s, Isaac Newton said the laws of nature he had discovered were so remarkable they pointed to the existence of a masterful creator. John Ray, an expert on plants and animals, wrote about the "wisdom of God" he saw in nature. In the 1800s, Michael Faraday and James Maxwell made major discoveries in electricity and magnetism. For both, the Bible was the basis of their faith, and their belief in a creator inspired their science. This does not mean science and faith are always in harmony. The way someone uses a scientific discovery might go against another person's religious view of right and wrong. Or someone might claim that only science can give us trustworthy knowledge. That goes against much religious thinking. These occasions can spark important and sometimes heated discussion. But the idea that science and religious faith are always at war is definitely false.

Q97

many
ientists
lieve in
d today?

f. Elaine
ward Ecklund,
ciologist;
f. Bob Thomson,
ciologist

There are scientists all around the world who believe in God or a higher power. We have spent several years asking scientists in eight different countries if they believe in God. In the UK 33 out of every 100 scientists said they believe in God. In India it was 78 and in Turkey it was 85.

Whether or not they believe in God, scientists can still have opinions about religion. Some think science and religion are in a battle, and if asked to choose, they would pick science. One third of UK scientists think this way. But many others see science and religion as partners working together – even some who don't have a personal faith. I talked to one UK scientist who knows lots about physics. He said that the beauty he sees in scientific discoveries, and the way science helps humanity, show him lots about the existence and character of God. He is just one example of a scientist who believes in God today.

Why doesn't the Bible talk about science like the Big Bang, evolution or dinosaurs?

Dr John H. Walton,
Old Testament
Theologian

I don't think the Bible is a book about everything, but one that reveals God's plans and purposes for humans. I believe God communicated His message to people who lived long ago based on what *they* knew and questions *they* asked. The Big Bang, evolution, and dinosaurs are things *we* know about and questions *we* have. Dinosaurs are exciting and interesting to us, but I don't think they are the key point in God's plans and purposes for humans. If God had included them in His messages, ancient Israelites would have had no idea what He was talking about.

I believe God knew what questions we would have, but He did not address all the questions every culture throughout time would have. I don't think the Bible is intended to be a science book, so it does not help us to understand science. It teaches us about God, presenting Him as the creator – active at every level. But it does not explain the mechanisms God used. I think exploring processes like evolution and the Big Bang is why God has given us the gift of science.

Will science eventually replace religious faith?

Prof. Rosalind Picard,
Computer Scientist
and Inventor

No. Science is brilliant, but it only deals with things that are observable and testable within space and time. Philosophy and religion go way beyond the scope of science. They deal with questions like: Why does anything exist at all? How come we can understand the universe? Why do we care about explanations, morals, and meanings? How do we know if a scientist is doing *good*? I think we need philosophy and religion to help us explore these important questions that science just can't find out.

Michael S.
dett,
ologian and
osopher

No, I don't think science could replace religion because they are different. But they're both important in telling us about our world. One might be more suitable than the other depending on the question you have. Science is great at telling us why we don't fly off the earth despite it spinning very fast (gravity). Religious faith is good at telling us why things matter and why we should love those around us. I think life and the universe are so amazing, big, and complicated that we need different ways to understand them. Science just can't explain it all.

Q100

hat is more
portant
r humanity:
ience or faith?

Elaine Storkey,
osopher and Social
entist

Science and faith are both important! I don't think one is more important than the other. Science helps us understand the world in amazing detail, including how human life exists alongside everything else. For example, through studying things like DNA, science has discovered how humans are related to other animals, insects, birds, and even bananas! Religious faith addresses questions about God as creator, the meaning and purpose of life, and how people interact, rightly or wrongly, with the rest of creation. So, science and faith are closely connected.

Climate change gives us an example. Science can measure things like rising temperatures, work out the impact of releasing greenhouse gasses, and show the disastrous effects of global warming on biodiversity and human life. Alongside science, Christian theology can explore what the Bible says about the world as a beautifully diverse creation, made by a loving creator God who gives humans the responsibility of caring for it. That can help us think about why we should do something to make it better.

I think it's best when we put faith and science together, to learn about, enjoy, sustain, protect, and preserve the world that I believe God has made.

What are the biggest challenges in the future of science and faith?

Prof. John Wyatt,
Medical Doctor and Ethicist

Prof. Rosalind Picard,
Computer Scientist and Inventor

Artificial intelligence (AI) is advancing so fast that it raises some very big questions for the future of humanity. Christianity teaches that human beings are special because they reflect the character of God, but if AI machines could do nearly everything as well as humans, and some things even better, then where would they fit? Would they also reflect God to the world? What would that mean for the way we treat them or what we use them to do or how we think about ourselves? There are many questions for us to think about!

Both science and religious faith are important parts of the age-old human quest to find out what's true and what's good. I think our biggest future challenges will be whatever gets in the way of that quest. The things that often get in the way are human pride, arrogance, selfishness, and fear. These can lead to people telling lies or making decisions that protect themselves but can harm others. So if we want to shape the world for the better, I think we need to make sure we are doing our best to be truthful, humble, brave, and kind in all we do.

Jennifer
Wiseman,
Astrophysicist

I think the challenge is for people to remember that science is not the right tool for all of our questions. Science is a wonderful tool for understanding the natural world, and answering questions about how it functions. Religious faith is better at addressing the bigger life issues of having a relationship with God, the purposes of our lives, how we should live, and how we might best use the amazing knowledge coming from science and technology.

Prof. Bill Newsome,
Neurobiologist

I believe the two biggest challenges in the future of science are taking care of our planet in an era of climate change, and understanding how our thoughts, emotions, and personalities come from the working of our brains. The biggest challenges in faith might be exactly the same! Can faith motivate us to use science to become better stewards of God's creation? And what might we ask or learn about God as a result of our growing understanding of how the brain works?

The Right Revd Prof.
N. T. Wright,
New Testament
Scholar

I think the biggest challenges for the future are the same as they have always been. Whatever new discoveries are made, we need to be careful how we use that knowledge. The Bible tells us we're an important part of God's bigger plan for the universe. I believe we get to experience the awe, wonder, and delight of exploring the universe and our relationship with God, but we also have a responsibility to look after these things well.

Meet the Contributors

Dr Althea Wilkinson: Astronomer; Domain Specialist, University of Manchester Square Kilometre Array Group: Questions 4, 8, 94, and Chapter 3 "Getting Personal"
Althea was part of a space mission which mapped the sky at the very beginning of the universe. She loves helping people to think about Big Questions like "Why are we here?".

The Revd Dr Andrew Davison: Theologian and Scientist; Starbridge Lecturer in Theology and Natural Sciences, University of Cambridge; Fellow in Theology and Dean of Chapel, Corpus Christi College, Cambridge: Question 34
Andrew loves science and theology, and got a PhD in both. He spent a year in the USA, on a scheme funded by NASA, thinking about what life elsewhere in the universe would mean for us.

Dr Andrew B. Torrance: Theologian; Lecturer in Theology, University of St Andrews: Questions 9, 11, and 15
Andrew studies God and all that God has planned for creation. He also loves the sciences and enjoys teaching people about what it means for scientists to study God's creation.

Andy Fletcher: Science Communicator; President of Life, the Universe and Everything: Questions 32 and 36
Andy Fletcher has talked to young people from 43 countries about things like black holes, the Big Bang, Quantum Cats, Slits, Tunnels, Tangles, Life, the Universe, and Everything! Plus God.

Dr April Maskiewicz Cordero: Biologist; Professor of Biology, Point Loma Nazarene University, San Diego, California: Questions 47, 68, and 92
In addition to teaching university students, April also travels a lot speaking to audiences about drawing together evolution and Christian faith.

Dr Beth Singler: Anthropologist; Junior Research Fellow in AI, Homerton College, University of Cambridge: Question 48
Beth is an anthropologist who thinks about what people think about machines that might think.

Dr Bethany Sollereder FRSA: Theologian; Postdoctoral Fellow in Science and Religion, University of Oxford: Question 81
Bethany loves reading and riding horses but spends most of her time thinking and teaching about the Big Questions of life: God, meaning, life, and death.

Meet the Contributors

▶ **Prof. Bill Newsome: Neurobiologist; Director of the Wu Tsai Neurosciences Institute; Professor of Neurobiology, Stanford University:** Questions 21 and 101
Bill studied physics as an undergraduate student and did a PhD in neurobiology. He explores how the visual parts of our brains enable us to see, and the brain mechanisms that enable us to make decisions.

▶ **Prof. Bob Thomson: Sociologist; Assistant Professor, The University of Alabama, Huntsville:** Question 97
Bob teaches criminology and sociology. Before becoming a sociologist, he worked as an engineer and studied theology, which is he is particularly interested in learning about how religion impacts our world – including science.

▶ **Prof. Bob White FRS: Geophysicist; Director of The Faraday Institute for Science and Religion; Professor of Geophysics, University of Cambridge:** Questions 12 and 66
Bob studies how volcanoes work and visits them when they are erupting! He enjoys helping people think about our responsibility to look after the planet he believes God made.

▶ **Cara Parrett: Marine Biologist; previously head of marine programmes for an NGO in the Republic of Maldives:** Question 72 and Chapter 6 "Getting Personal"
Cara is a Christian and a scientist. She has studied the ocean since she grew up in South Africa, and now she wants to protect the animals living under the surface by helping people care for God's creation.

▶ **Prof. Cara Wall-Scheffler: Anthropologist; Professor of Biology, Seattle Pacific University:** Questions 13, 43, and 70
Cara got her PhD from the University of Cambridge, where she studied how Neanderthals hunted and what resources they used right before the last ice age. Now she studies how both living people and extinct groups – like Neanderthals – walk, run, jump, and carry their children.

▶ **Dr David Lahti: Behavioural Biologist; Professor of Biology at Queens College, City University of New York:** Questions 19, 76, and 77
David grew up loving nature and the wilderness. Now he studies it and teaches college students about it. He especially enjoys investigating how birds and humans learn and behave.

▶ **The Revd Prof. David Wilkinson BSc, PhD, MA, PhD, FRAS: Astrophysicist and Theologian; Professor and Principal of St John's College in the Department of Theology and Religion, Durham University:** Questions 3, 5, 31, 61, and Chapter 8 "Getting Started"
David Wilkinson is an astrophysicist who teaches science and Christianity at Durham University. He loves Star Wars, The Simpsons, and Newcastle United.

Dr Deb Haarsma: Astrophysicist; President of Biologos; previously Professor and Chair of the Department of Physics and Astronomy at Calvin College: Questions 7 and 10
Deb Haarsma loves studying galaxies far across the universe, and thinking about how astronomy fits with her Christian faith. She has used telescopes all over Earth and telescopes in space. She and her husband enjoy science fiction and classical music.

Dr Denis Alexander: Biochemist; Director Emeritus, The Faraday Institute for Science and Religion: Questions 39, 82, and Chapter 8 "Getting Personal"
Denis has spent nearly his whole life in scientific research, first on the brain, then on disease-causing genes, and then on the ways in which we defend ourselves against bacteria and viruses. He also spent 15 years in the Middle East teaching science in universities.

Dr Dennis Venema: Geneticist; Professor of Biology at Trinity Western University, British Columbia: Question 38
Dennis enjoys teaching evolutionary biology to his students and exploring how individual biological cells connect to form the tissues that living things are made of.

Prof. Elaine Howard Ecklund: Sociologist; Director of Religion and Public Life Program and Professor of Sociology, Rice University: Question 97
Elaine teaches sociology. She has travelled to several countries in order to ask scientists what they think about religion. She uses their answers to dispel myths about religion and science.

Dr Elaine Storkey: Philosopher and Social Scientist, broadcaster and writer; Former lecturer in Divinity at University of Oxford and Kings College London: Questions 89 and 100
Elaine has travelled across many parts of Africa and Haiti visiting schools and listening to questions about faith.

Dr Elspeth Darley: Psychologist and Theologian: Questions 41 and 57
By day Elspeth helps people with mental health problems in the hospital. By night she loves exploring where the Bible came from and whether we can trust it.

Dr Emily Burdett: Developmental Psychologist; Assistant Professor of Psychology, University of Nottingham: Questions 64, 65, and 77
Emily studies how children think and learn. She likes to ask them questions about how they understand other people, God, and the world around them.

Prof. Eric Priest: Mathematician; Professor of Mathematics at St Andrews University: Question 16
Eric uses maths to develop theories that help us understand puzzling fundamental processes that we observe in the universe, especially on our sun. He has long been interested in the links between science and faith.

▶ **The Revd Dr Ernest Lucas: Biblical Scholar; Vice-Principal Emeritus, Bristol Baptist College:** Question 42 and Chapter 5 "Getting Started"
Ernest taught biblical studies at Bristol Baptist College and Bristol University. He is now retired but still enjoys helping people to read the Bible and understand what it teaches.

▶ **Dr Francis S. Collins MD, PhD: Physician and Geneticist; Director of the National Institutes of Health (NIH):** Questions 22, 37, 47, 94, and Chapter 4 "Getting Personal"
Francis led the Human Genome Project which produced the first finished sequence of human DNA. He has served under two US Presidents as Director of the NIH, and received the Presidential Medal of Freedom and the National Medal of Science. Francis became a Christian during his medical training, and founded the BioLogos Foundation, which helps people think about how science and Christian faith go together.

▶ **George Hawker: Astrophysicist; PhD Student, University of Cambridge:** Question 30
George has always been crazy about space. He still wants to be an astronaut when he grows up! At the moment he uses some of the biggest telescopes in the world to explore "exoplanet atmospheres" – that means looking at what's in the air around planets outside our solar system.

▶ **The Revd Dr Gillian Straine: Physicist and Theologian; CEO of The Guild of Health and St Raphael:** Questions 53, 62, and Chapter 7 "Getting Started"
Gillian had great fun flying around Australian storm systems when she was getting a PhD in physics. She is an ordained priest and now runs a charity which helps people think about health and healing.

▶ **Dr Hannah Earnshaw: Astronomer; Postdoctoral Researcher, Space Radiation Laboratory, Caltech:** Questions 28, 35, and 59
Hannah is an X-ray astronomer who dreams of one day living on Mars! They use telescopes in orbit around Earth to find out what happens around black holes and neutron stars.

▶ **Hannah Pagel: Astronomer; Science Teacher at Mountain Academy of Teton Science Schools; Stargazing Leader for Wyoming Stargazing:** Questions 1, 25, and Chapter 3 "Getting Started"
Hannah has worked on a Mars rover, discovered new galaxies, and studied everything in between! Now, she shares what she's learned while leading stargazing programs and teaching middle school and high school science in and around Grand Teton National Park (Wyoming, USA).

▶ **Prof. Hasok Chang: Philosopher; Hans Rausing Professor of History and Philosophy of Science, University of Cambridge:** Question 91
Hasok loved physics as a student but became a philosopher as he found himself asking questions about science that scientists didn't seem to want to think about. He now enjoys helping scientists and others think about those questions.

▶ **Prof. Hugh Rollinson: Geochemist; Course Director, The Faraday Institute for Science and Religion; Emeritus Professor of Earth Sciences, University of Derby:** Questions 14 and 67
Hugh studies Earth's oldest rocks. He grinds his samples to a powder in order to be able to chemically analyse them. These results help us think about our origins.

▶ **Dr J. Richard Middleton: Theologian; Professor of Biblical Worldview and Exegesis, Northeastern Seminary at Roberts Wesleyan College, Rochester, New York:** Question 44
J. Richard Middleton is a Jamaican living in the USA, who teaches the Bible to university students and people who want to be pastors or priests in the church.

▶ **James D. Torrance: Primary School Student:** Question 11
James is a primary school student who, like his dad Andrew, loves exploring what we can know about the universe we live in, as he believes it has been created by God.

▶ **Prof. Jeff Hardin: Developmental Biologist; Professor, Department of Integrative Biology, University of Wisconsin-Madison:** Question 78
Jeff Hardin is a biology professor and a Christian. He uses powerful microscopes to study how fertilized eggs grow to become animals.

▶ **Dr Jennifer Wiseman: Astrophysicist; Director of the American Association for the Advancement of Science's Dialogue on Science, Ethics, and Religion; previously Head of the Goddard Laboratory for Exoplanets and Stellar Astrophysics:** Questions 6, 29, 101, and Chapter 1 "Getting Personal"
Dr Jennifer Wiseman is a scientist who studies space using different kinds of telescopes to observe galaxies, stars, comets, and planets. She loves animals, nature, and looking up at the night sky. She even discovered a comet which is named after her!

▶ **The Revd Dr Joanna Collicutt: Neuropsychologist and Theologian; Karl Jaspers Lecturer in Psychology and Spirituality at Ripon College, Cuddesdon; Oxford Diocesan Advisor for Spiritual Care for Older People:** Questions 13, 37, 87, and 94
Joanna studies what makes people feel happy and upset and uses this to try and help them feel more like themselves. She also likes helping people feel happy by baking them delicious cakes!

▶ **Prof. John Bryant: Geneticist and Bioethicist; Professor Emeritus of Cell and Molecular Biology and former Head of Biosciences at Exeter University:** Question 18
Prof. John Bryant spent many years doing research on genes and DNA. He is also interested in ethics (thinking about what is right and what is wrong) in science, medicine, and in our relationship with the natural world.

Prof. John Hedley Brooke: Historian of Science; Retired Professor of Science and Religion, University of Oxford: Question 96
As a youngster John enjoyed the smells and colours of chemistry, which he studied at Cambridge. He then became a historian of science, fascinated by the lives of scientists, including their religious beliefs.

Dr John H. Walton: Old Testament Theologian; Professor of Old Testament, Wheaton College: Question 98
John teaches and writes books about the Bible's Old Testament, especially how we can understand it better when we use information from the ancient world.

Prof. John Wyatt: Medical Doctor and Ethicist; Emeritus Professor of Neonatal Paediatrics, Ethics and Perinatology, University College London: Questions 51, 90, 101, and Chapter 7 "Getting Personal"
John worked for many years as a doctor for babies and a research scientist, developing new ways of protecting babies' brains from damage. Now he is trying to make sure that artificial intelligence is used for the good of human beings everywhere.

Dr Jonathan Moo: Ecologist and Theologian; Associate Professor of New Testament and Environmental Studies, Whitworth University: Questions 13 and 56
Jonathan writes and teaches about the Bible and the natural world. His favourite thing is to take students into the mountains to explore and study and worship God together.

Dr Joseph Tennant: Psychologist; previously Post-Doctoral researcher on "Mystical Seizures in Epilepsy", University of Cambridge: Question 24
Joseph studies how people experience religion and how it impacts their beliefs and morality. He likes to discover how people come to believe things, and how belief can change the world!

Prof. Justin L. Barrett: Developmental Psychologist; Chief Project Developer, Office for Science, Theology, and Religion Initiatives, Fuller Theological Seminary: Questions 46, 62, and Chapter 6 "Getting Started"
Justin studies how children and adults think and learn, especially about God. He loves thinking about how scientific discoveries can help people thrive.

Dr Katharine Hayhoe: Climate Scientist; Professor of Political Science and Director of Climate Centre, Texas Tech University; CEO of the consulting firm ATMOS Research and Consulting: Question 20 and Chapter 2 "Getting Personal"
Katharine studies how climate change affects people, animals, and plants around the world, and what we can do to fix it.

Prof. Malcolm Jeeves CBE, FRSE, FMedSci: Psychologist; Emeritus Professor of Psychology, University of St Andrews; formerly President of The Royal Society of Edinburgh: Question 45
Malcolm studies how brains work. He looks at how damage in different parts of the brain affects how we think, feel, and act. His work helps him think about what the Bible means when it says we are "wonderfully made" by God.

Dr Margaret W. Miller: Marine Ecologist; Research Director, SECORE International: Question 73
Margaret works to restore coral reefs as she believes that God loves corals and created coral reefs as a beautiful part of the natural system which sustains all living things, including humans. Her favourite animals are corals and cuttlefish.

Prof. Mary Higby Schweitzer: Palaeontologist; Professor, Department of Biological Sciences, North Carolina State University; Associate Researcher, Museum of the Rockies, Montana State University: Question 71
Mary's brother introduced her to dinosaurs when she was only five years old. He gave her books about them, like her favourite, *The Enormous Egg* (by Oliver Butterworth). She never outgrew her fascination for those ancient beasts and now studies them, discovering amazing things that are changing how we think about dinosaurs, fossils, and the world.

Dr Matt Pritchard: Physicist and Magician; Associate of the Inner Magic Circle: Question 58
Matt is a magician, scientist, and professional speaker. He loves discovering the wonders of the world through studying, playing, and exploring things from Lego to lasers. He also loves sharing them with his daughters, school groups, and everyone else!

Dr Michael S. Burdett: Theologian and Philosopher; Assistant Professor of Christian Theology, University of Nottingham; Associate of the Ian Ramsey Centre for Science and Religion, Oxford: Questions 48, 52, and 99
Michael studies how Christians think about the future and how science and technology has and should influence that.

Dr Michael J. Murray: Philosopher; Senior Visiting Scholar in Philosophy, Franklin and Marshall College: Question 84
Michael studies ways that science can help us to better understand God and creation. He writes articles and gives talks to students and adults who sometimes have a hard time understanding how science and Christian faith can fit together.

Meet the Contributors

Dr Nick Higgs: Marine Biologist; Director of the Cape Eleuthera Institute, The Bahamas: Question 74
Nick studies animals that live in the oceans, especially lobsters and worms. He works with fishermen to help them look after the oceans.

Nick Spencer: Historian of Ideas; Senior Fellow, Theos: Questions 63, 65, and 93
Nick researches religion in Britain today, particularly thinking about what people believe, what they don't believe – and why they do and don't believe it!

Prof. Paul Copan: Theologian and Philosopher; Palm Beach Atlantic University, Florida: Question 88
Prof. Paul likes to tell people how Jesus is the answer to life's biggest questions. Sometimes he includes lots of details to help them think about these questions. He also likes looking at birds and photographing them.

Prof. Paul Fairchild: Stem Cell Biologist; Fellow of Trinity College, Oxford; Founding Director of the Oxford Stem Cell Institute; Associate Professor, Sir William Dunn School of Pathology, University of Oxford: Questions 17 and 95
Paul studies stem cells and the unique way in which they heal and rejuvenate ageing tissues, a topic he considers to be more urgent as he gets older!

Dr Rhoda J. Hawkins: Biological Physicist; Senior Lecturer in Biological Physics Theory, University of Sheffield: Questions 15, 17, and 80
Rhoda is a lecturer in physics at the University of Sheffield. In her research she works with other scientists on how biological cells move and change shape.

Dr Robert Sluka: Marine Biologist; Marine and Coastal Conservation Programme, A Rocha International: Question 19
Robert studies the ocean and how it connects us to God, each other, and all the creatures that live in it.

The Revd Dr Rodney Holder FRAS, FIMA: Cosmologist and Theologian; Emeritus Course Director, The Faraday Institute for Science and Religion: Questions 2, 54, and 90
Rodney studies how our amazing universe is put together and how it points to God, who he believes made it all. As a church minister he loves telling people about God's love for us shown in Jesus.

The Revd Dr Roger P. Abbott: Practical Theologian; Senior Research Associate in Natural Disasters, The Faraday Institute for Science and Religion, Cambridge: Question 83
Roger studies big natural disasters and the impact they have on people. He enjoys helping young people think about these events and, hopefully, become as excited as he is about showing how people can prevent disasters happening.

Dr Roger Bretherton: Psychologist; Associate Professor, School of Psychology, University of Lincoln: Question 86
Roger does research on what makes us better people, asking questions like, "Does being thankful make us happier?" and "How can we make wise choices?".

Prof. Rosalind Picard: Computer Scientist and Inventor; Member of the National Academy of Engineering; Professor of Media Arts and Sciences; Founder and Director, Affective Computing Research Group; Faculty Chair, MIT MindHandHeart: Questions 50, 99, 101, and Chapter 4 "Getting Started"
Rosalind is an inventor who also studies how the human brain processes information. She helps to develop machines with artificial intelligence that can help to improve people's health through understanding emotion.

Dr Sarah Bodbyl Roels: Evolutionary Biologist; Faculty Developer, Colorado School of Mines: Questions 27, 69, and Chapter 2 "Getting Started"
Sarah is a biologist who studies the fascinating lives of plants and animals and helps university professors teach their students. She loves studying God's word and God's world and helping others learn more about both.

Sarah Walker: Environmental Communicator; International Coordinator, A Rocha International: Question 27
Sarah helps conservation teams around the world by connecting people and spreading the word about caring for creation. She loves being outside, especially walking under trees and by the sea.

Prof. Simon Conway Morris FRS: Biologist; Emeritus Professor of Evolutionary Palaeobiology, University of Cambridge: Questions 40 and 75
Simon started collecting fossils when he was about eight and since then his interests have grown and grown. As far as he is concerned, that there is no end to the things to discover is the best possible news.

Prof. Stephanie Clarke: Neuroscientist; Professor and Head of the Neuropsychology and Neurorehabilitation Clinic at the University Hospital, Lausanne, Switzerland: Questions 22 and 55
Stephanie is a physician, and head of a clinic which provides rehabilitation like speech therapy to patients with serious brain trauma. Stephanie is especially interested in researching how certain parts of our brains can change.

Prof. Stephen Freeland: Astrobiologist; Director of Interdisciplinary Studies at the University of Maryland, Baltimore, USA: Questions 27 and 33
Stephen is a Christian who studied zoology, computer science, and genetics and ended up focusing upon the earliest evolution of life on our planet. He has worked with NASA and enjoys researching what life elsewhere in the universe might be like.

Dr Steve Roels: Environmental Biologist: Questions 43 and 49
Steve is a conservation biologist who studies how planting trees creates habitats for tropical forest birds and how those birds protect the trees by eating insects.

Dr Susan D. Benecchi: Planetary Astronomer; Senior Scientist, Planetary Science Institute, Herndon, Virginia: Questions 14 and 26
Susan uses telescopes to better understand the nature and character of God through the world she believes He created. She homeschools her children and loves talking about how God's truths are relevant to their lives.

Prof. Tim O'Connor: Philosopher; Professor of Philosophy and member of the Cognitive Sciences Program, Indiana University, Bloomington: Question 85
Tim spends his days thinking about Big Questions about the human mind and God – alone, with his college students, or with other scholars. Then he writes down his ideas.

Dr Tom Ingleby: Geophysicist; previously PhD student in the Institute of Geophysics and Tectonics, Leeds University: Question 80 and Chapter 5 "Getting Personal"
Tom watches the earth bend, squash, and shake from space using satellites. He became a Christian at university whilst studying geology and loves thinking about big questions in science and faith.

Prof. Tom McLeish: Theoretical Physicist; Professor of Natural Philosophy, University of York: Questions 60, and Chapter 1 "Getting Started"
Tom McLeish is a scientist working on the physics that happens inside living cells. He is also interested in how people create new ideas in both art and science, and in how the Bible shows us the reasons for finding out about nature.

Prof. Tom Shakespeare FBA: Sociologist, Broadcaster, and Social Influencer; Professor of Disability Research at the London School of Hygiene and Tropical Medicine: Questions 37 and 80
Tom spends his time talking to disabled people in Africa and Asia and trying to discover what works to make their lives go better.

The Right Revd Prof. Dr N. T. Wright DD, FRSE: New Testament Scholar; Professor of New Testament and Early Christianity, University of St Andrews; previously Bishop of Durham: Questions 23, 79, 93, and 101
Tom (N. T.) Wright likes to think about what the Bible can tell us. He has written over 80 books and broadcasts frequently on radio and television.

Glossary

Artificial intelligence: a computer program, made by people, that lets machines perform tasks that seem intelligent, like speaking, composing music, or learning.

Atoms: tiny building blocks of chemical **elements**.

Black hole: a part of the universe where **gravity** is so strong that everything close is pulled in, including light.

Cells: biological building blocks making up all the parts of living things – eyes, muscles, skin, blood, leaves, etc. Each tiny cell is wrapped in a very thin outer layer (membrane) and contains DNA and lots of other important bits and pieces.

Climate Change: long-term change in the general weather and temperature of an area or the whole world.

Dark matter: mysterious **matter** that can't be detected directly, but is thought to exist because it seems to do things like help hold stars in orbit in their galaxies.

DNA: Deoxyribonucleic acid – a special **molecule** in the **cells** of living things containing an instruction code for some of how the living thing grows and behaves.

Element: a pure chemical substance (like hydrogen, gold or oxygen) made only of its own specific type of **atom**.

Gene: a section of **DNA** containing the instruction code for a particular feature.

General Relativity: Einstein's **theory** of **gravity**, including ideas about **black holes** and the way that space and time can be bent by **matter.**

Gravity: an invisible force that pulls objects with **mass** towards other objects with **mass** (like a ball towards the ground). Gravity does some amazing and weird things like actually bending space and time!

Jesus: Christians believe that God is three 'persons' in one – the 'Father', the 'Son' (Jesus), and the 'Holy Spirit'. The Bible teaches that Jesus came to Earth, lived, and died as a human, and came back to life again, so that people could know God fully.

Mass: the amount of **matter** in an object (often measured in grams or kilograms). The weight of an object is different as it depends on **gravity**, so you would weigh different amounts on different-sized planets, even though your mass would be the same!

Matter: any substance that has **mass** and takes up space (even really small things).

Miracle: an extraordinary or unusual event, believed to be caused by God or something else supernatural.

Molecule: joined-up **atoms** forming the smallest amount of a substance. For example, two hydrogen **atoms** joined to one oxygen **atom** make a water molecule – the smallest possible amount of water!

Particles: tiny bits making up all **matter** – like electrons, protons, and neutrons that **atoms** are made of, and the tinier bits (like quarks) that make *them* up.

Resurrection: coming back to life from the dead (often used to talk about Jesus).

Space-time: physics has shown that space and time are connected in the way they are affected by things like **gravity**, so we talk about 'space-time' to describe how they interact.

Special Relativity: a **theory** started by Einstein to explain strange things that happen when an object and someone watching it are moving relative to one another – like lengths seeming shorter and time slowing down.

Species: a group of closely related living things that can have healthy babies together, which can then grow up to have their own healthy babies.

Theory (scientific): a carefully thought out explanation of experimental findings and observations about a particular aspect of the natural world.

Index

If you enjoyed exploring these Great Big Questions, remember to check out **www.faradaykids.com** for more questions and answers, as well as activities, videos, and more about our other resources all about science, God, and Big Questions!

Picture credits
All illustrations and artwork by Andy Rowland except:

Getty
pp. 11 (Lemon_tm); 14 (arvitalya); 18 (hadzi3); 24 (SDI Productions); 31 (tatarnikova); 34 (loops7); 38 (Elen11); 42 (Mikhail Leonov); 51 (gorodenkoff); 54 (Sasiistock); 63 (appledesign); 69 (lucentius); 72 (rdonar); 74 (freedom007); 82 (IMPALASTOCK); 88 (kadirdemir); 92 (Nekan); 94 (alexeys); 96 (BrianAJackson); 103 (shironosov)

Unsplash
pp. 26 (master-wen); 30 (greg-rakozy); 58 (alex-knight)